RICHARD WRIGHT

RICHARD WRIGHT
Impressions and Perspectives

Edited by
David Ray and Robert M. Farnsworth
Introduction by Charles T. Davis

Ann Arbor Paperbacks
THE UNIVERSITY OF MICHIGAN PRESS

First edition as an Ann Arbor Paperback 1973

ISBN 0–472–09189–1 (clothbound)
ISBN 0–472–06189–5 (paperbound)
Published in the United States of America by
The University of Michigan Press and simultaneously
in Don Mills, Canada, by Longman Canada Limited
Manufactured in the United States of America

The material reprinted in this book first appeared
in the December, 1971, issue of *New Letters,* Volume 38,
Number 2. Permissions requests should be addressed to
the Editor of *New Letters,* University of Missouri-
Kansas City, Kansas City, Missouri 64110.

The photograph of Richard Wright in Chicago was furnished by Michel Fabre. The Wading River photograph came from Frances McClernan. The movie stills of *Native Son* were provided by Irwin T. Holtzman and by Thomas Cripps, who furnished the mats of the movie. Lloyd J. Reynolds's calligraphy of Richard Wright's haiku is used with Mrs. Ellen Wright's permission. The sheet music and lyrics to "King Joe" are used with permission of Hansen Publications of Miami Beach, Florida, and of Bregman, Vocco and Conn, Inc. The line from Tu Fu, calligraphed by Lloyd J. Reynolds and used with permission of Harvard University Press, is adapted from William Hung's translation in *Tu Fu: China's Greatest Poet.*

Dedicated to Richard & Ellen Wright

A fame
that is to last
a thousand years
will rise after
an unappreciated life
is past

TU FU

Preface

We are happy to have a gracious and incisive introduction by Charles T. Davis to add to this reprinting of our special issue of *New Letters* on Richard Wright. We are also happy to acknowledge the seminal influence of the Richard Wright Institute held at the University of Iowa during the summer of 1971.

Beyond that we need to acknowledge the special support of three individuals. Professor Davis, besides writing an introduction, was instrumental in our securing the three pieces from the institute by Aaron, Fabre, and Walker. At the institute and since, Michel Fabre has been an invaluable supportive resource for our special issue on Richard Wright. Professor Fabre of the Sorbonne has been working in Paris with Wright manuscript material for many years. He is a close and insightful reader and a warm and engaging man. It is through him and through the confidence Ellen Wright has come to have in him that we have been able to obtain the unpublished Richard Wright manuscript on racial prejudice as well as the previously unpublished letters to Richard Wright by contemporary writers. Our debt to Michel Fabre is only one of many in a growing list compiled by Wright students and scholars.

Ellen Wright, who continues to live in Paris, has also been extremely generous. We are grateful to her for permission to publish the Wright lecture, the letters to Wright, and the haiku.

CLA and *Studies in Black Literature* have previously done special issues on Richard Wright. The University of Iowa has now held a two-week summer institute on Richard Wright. Our issue is one more contribution to the continuing effort to realize the special nature of Richard Wright's achievement.

Richard Wright moved through the American experience with astonishing social and intellectual mobility. Born in Mississippi, he became a writer in Chicago, achieved literary prominence in New York, and linked the black American experience to international politics in Paris. He moved through fundamentalist Protestantism, Marxism, Existentialism, and showed interest in Orientalism. Throughout all of these experiences he was both *black* and *a man.* He insisted on his blackness although he pictured black life in America as inhuman and sterile. He raged against the racism of America and colonial Europe, but he seized the cultural tools of America and Europe with avidity and used them with power to open doors for himself and others who suffered from racism.

His writing became a powerful fist, but curled inside was a passionate human statement. He battered down doors, but he deeply appreciated grace, reason, truly humane civilization. He ever sought the comprehensive cultural picture which would illuminate the root causes of racism and lead to its elimination. He moved through a series of symbolic cities, but he never abandoned his ties with the past. He wrote letters from New York to Jackson, Mississippi. In Paris he kept his ties open with black America. His career was continuous and evolivng. He moved swiftly, but not carelessly. He traveled, but never away from himself.

It should surprise no one now that Richard Wright is claimed by so many as part of their own. He was one and many. The joy of this editorial opportunity is to put together many perspectives on Richard Wright, some clearly in sharp competition with others, but all finally implicitly a tribute to the vitality and achievement of a man who affirmed and challenged the human spirit in all of us.

ROBERT M. FARNSWORTH

Contents

Exile

Some Critical Commentary

Introduction

I like to think that this new collection of pieces by and about Richard Wright is the happy consequence of an institute run by the Program on Afro-American Studies at the University of Iowa during two hot weeks in July, 1971. If so, we have a demonstration that the academy is sometimes fertile, that an idea might be conceived, and profitably shared. This is not to say that the editors, Robert Farnsworth and David Ray, have relied heavily for the substance of this collection upon the Richard Wright Institute. Actually, they have used only three of seventeen papers delivered in July—by Michel Fabre, Daniel Aaron, and Margaret Walker Alexander. What the institute provided was the germ for this enterprise, the idea that Richard Wright somehow still lived in America, despite neglect by critics and readers, despite the reductive distortions of politics, and despite an extended and unbroken period of exile. Responding to the impulse nourished by the institute, the editors have put together an anthology which is both critical and creative. They have attached to reminiscences of friends and estimates of his achievement a selection of Wright's Haiku, a few from the large collection that remains largely untouched in Paris; Wright's blues ballad "King Joe," written for Paul Robeson with music by Count Basie; and a fine poetic tribute to Wright by Michael Harper, a contemporary black poet. All of these items point to the existence of one indisputable fact that the institute affirmed—that Wright was important to us again.

Despite the influence of several valuable books recently published, few writers have suffered as much as Wright has from reductive literary criticism. Perhaps, Dreiser has, in recent years, and Henry James before him. What obsesses most Americans is a pattern of events that is automatically attached to the name "Wright." It goes something like this. Richard was a sensitive black boy who survived, largely by luck, the dehumanizing oppression of the American South. He experienced a conversion to Communism in Chicago and disaffection with Communism in New York. In any event, a consequence of either or both was a period of expatriation in Paris, during which Wright became an existentialist and during which, as well, he ceased to count as a serious writer. This simple story has overtones that are either tragic or pathetic, depending upon how the teller of the tale estimates Wright's original talent. The underlying assumption here is that Wright's strength as a writer depended wholly upon the intense nearness of American experience and that the experience of expatriation deprived him, then, of his legitimate materials and signaled his end as an artist. That assumption is wrong, and the tale itself is not an uncommon instance of American provincialism posing as critical truth.

Equipped with this perspective, we are amazed to discover that the South of *Black Boy* is as much an artistic fabrication as it is an accurate record, a fact that disturbed W. E. B. Du Bois profoundly when the book appeared in 1945 ("Richard Wright Looks Back," New York *Herald Tribune Weekly* Book Review, March 4, 1945, p. 2). Daniel Aaron suggests in "Richard Wright and the Communist Party" that Wright's allegiance to Communism was always qualified—by his own irrepressible individualism and by his more basic commitment to art. We know too that his disaffection with Communism was similarly qualified—by his disinclination to attack Marxists in the age of Joseph McCarthy and by his continuing sense of an indebtedness to a Marxist view of history. Wright did not suffer a premature burial in Europe. His existentialism, as Michel Fabre points out in

"Richard Wright and the French Existentialists" (an essay delivered at the Richard Wright Institute), is homegrown, not a faddist acquisition, detectable, perhaps as early as "Down by the Riverside" in *Uncle Tom's Children* (1938), and his fiction, as Katherine Sprandel demonstrates here in her discussion of Wright's last novel, *The Long Dream* (1958), displays a continuing preoccupation with themes that are projected fully first in *Native Son* (1940). There is no disjunction in his work, though we may expect to find one. There is perhaps a decline in power in the 1950s but no break in the unity of his imagination. What emerges in the fiction is the record of an unusual internal journey, surprisingly bleak and solitary, involving components of action that change in meaning and in level of importance—elements like deprivation, self-deception, violence, flight, and self-awareness.

Nor did Wright's departure from the Communist party and his residence in France mark any cessation in political activity. Wright became involved with Sartre in organizing and promoting the non-Communist left, a movement called Rassemblement Démocratique Révolutionnaire. This was an effort to provide an alternative to choosing up sides between the Soviet Union and the United States of America as they faced each other in the Cold War. When this political phenomenon of the late forties disintegrated, torn by dissension and factionalism, Wright turned his attention to the emerging African republics, retaining the conception of a political role that might develop outside of the orbits of influence of the two great powers. Despite these exotic commitments Wright remained thoroughly American. Baldwin sensed this fact when he commented in *Nobody Knows My Name* (New York: Dell Publishing Company, Inc., 1961, p. 48) on Wright's difficulties in addressing the Conference of Negro-African Writers and Artists in Paris in September, 1956. Wright's devotion to the European Enlightenment, his notion that it was good for Africans to be freed from the "rot" of their past, seemed strange to Baldwin, at least in a gathering of black artists largely from Africa and the West Indies. Certainly the most eloquent statement of the persistence of his Americanism is to be found in Michel Fabre's article in this volume, "Wright's Exile." Here Fabre records Wright's definitions of an American, definitions strongly influenced by the language and the habit of incremental repetition often associated with Wright's sister expatriate, Gertrude Stein. Typical is "I am an American but I insist upon talking about the meaning of being an American because I know that being an American means more to the world and mankind than what is defined as being an American today." Wright remained an intensely political animal to the end of his life. In his Paris years he experienced political challenges undreamed of in Chicago and New York, trials that forced a development in the subtlety of this political thought and the power of his rhetoric.

Wright was rediscovered by the angry blacks of the late sixties. Cleaver put down Baldwin and elevated Wright, and we have a case of the destruction of the intellectual father by the rebellious son. I should say "again," since Baldwin had attacked Wright earlier, and for very much the same reason. Baldwin complains in "Many Thousands Gone" in *Notes of a Native Son* (Boston: Beacon Press, 1955, p. 39) of the absence of "any sense of Negro life as a continuing and complex group reality" in *Native Son.* Cleaver counters in *Soul on Ice* (New York: McGraw-Hill Book Company, 1968, p. 108), by observing that Wright "reigns supreme for his profound political, economic, and social reference" and adds that Wright "had the ability, like Dreiser, of harnessing the gigantic, overwhelming forces and focussing them, with pinpoint sharpness, on individuals and their acts...." Indeed, Cleaver insists, "it is Baldwin's work which is so void of a political, economic, or even a social reference." What appears to be a standoff, as Morris Dickstein shrewdly observes in "Wright, Baldwin, Cleaver," is not. The burden of truth is with the most recent rebel—Cleaver—who has refused to be taken in by the murky formalism of Baldwin's early criticism.

With an accurate perspective on the cultural climate of the times, Dickstein sees another reason for Wright's return to grace —indeed, to put the question more accurately, for his enduring power. *Black Boy,* for Dickstein, enunciates "a fundamental pattern of black writing, that of the 'Bildungsroman.' " It provides a model for the narrative dramatizing the evolution and the liberation of the consciousness of a black man and a form that repeats itself again and again in the years that follow—in *Invisible Man, The Autobiography of Malcolm X,* Cleaver's *Soul on Ice,* and, most recently, George Cain's novel *Blueschild Baby.* We should not forget, in acknowledging Wright's greatness in *Black Boy,* that his strength rests upon foundations of earlier wonder erected by Joyce and Dostoevski as well as upon his own naked view of the reality in the American South.

Dickstein comments upon Wright's mastery of the mind "in extremis" with appropriate documentation from *Native Son,* but he does not see how this competence gives Wright a special position in our time. The step from the extreme to the absurd, from values in profound conflict to no fixed values at all, from conventional artistic structures to grotesque forms of organization is a very short one. Wright seems poised to take that step at the end of *Native Son.* He does move forward, with many reservations, in *The Outsider* (1953), and, doing so, he joins the company of the writers of grotesque fiction of the fifties—Ellison, Mailer, Bowles, Hawkes, Styron, Heller, Barth, and Flannery O'Connor the makers of the literary consciousness in the fiction of our world. Understanding Wright may be a simple way of getting to know modern achievement in fiction since he marches so deliberately through the transition from the limits of naturalism to the edge of the grotesque.

This collection of pieces, edited by Ray and Farnsworth, has revealed something of Wright's inner vitality, the talent that is once again close to us. Beyond this, it shows Wright's wide-ranging creative interests, not just in the literary forms to which he could bring a rare intensity. We are provided with an intimation of what Fanon was referring to in a letter dated January 6, 1953, from Hôpital Psychiatrique de Saint-Alban (Lozère) to Wright when he spoke with respect of the "human breadth" of his works.

CHARLES T. DAVIS

A Posthumously Published Essay

The American Problem—Its Negro Phase

RICHARD WRIGHT

Note by Michel Fabre: This is an unfinished first draft of an essay written in the early fifties, which was being prepared for delivery to a French audience, and accounts for the abruptness with which it ends. The essay is used here with the gracious permission of Mrs. Ellen Wright.

In the realms of religion and literature the US Negro has long sought to influence the conscience of the US white toward a more liberal treatment of his people. So far, he has failed; but where he failed another and more powerful force, cynical and irresistible, has in a small but significant measure succeeded. That state of tension and pressure which has now existed for some five years between the USA and the USSR has caused American whites to experience a deep sense of guilt and uneasiness in relation to her 15,000,000-strong Negro minority. Arraigned by Communist propaganda as a racist and exploiter before the bar of world opinion, the USA has moved, clumsily and reluctantly to be sure, to ease the educational, housing and job discrimination against men and women of color.

How did this happen? What is its background? What was it that moved whites when America's own sacred documents failed to do so? Was it love of mankind, of minorities, of justice? Or was it just plain hysterical fear and self-interest?

Traditionally, the "Negro problem" was considered a sectional one, namely a Southern problem, and Southern whites fought jealously to keep it so, referring to "our colored folks," a peculiar race who had to live apart from the rest of mankind. Even in the broadest and most liberal sense, the "Negro problem" was referred to as America's problem, a mere matter of adjusting and accommodating people who were completely alien in blood and skin. Any one who raised the "Negro problem" in its deepest human sense was vaguely regarded as a crusader, sometimes even a trouble-maker, an unbalanced n'er-do-well who evoked imaginary social and racial evils to detract from his own lack of personal success.

Happily all of this is now past.

During World War I, the US had used a set of rigidly racist rules to "keep Negroes in their place." In that day US whites had but few militant Negroes to contend with. W.E.B. DuBois, Monroe Trotter, Walter White, etc. have sharply condemned white racism but to little avail. Whites of the USA successfully fought the Kaiser and defeated him without so much as feeling one iota of contradiction between the Negroes they oppressed and the so-called "plight of the Belgian babies."

When World War II broke out, with Japanese attacks in the Pacific and German attacks in the Atlantic, US whites trotted out their moth-eaten racial rules of World War I and tried to put them into practice. They did not count upon the hard fact that the Negro of World War II was not the same Negro they had so easily handled during World War I.

The quarter of a century which separated World War I from World War II had witnessed a qualitative change in the status and consciousness of the US Negro. He was more intelligent, more widely travelled, more widely read, better trained, healthier, and had been swept by the CIO and radical labor activity into hundreds of thousands of trade union jobs. The Negro press had grown immensely. Negro literary expression had surged upward by leaps and bounds and a bedrock sense of class-consciousness had come to give backbone to Negro decisions and actions, as shown in the A. Philip Randolph March on Washington movement.

Naturally the rigid rules of World War I could not contain the energies and aspirations of such a people. Riots broke out in Beaumont, Texas, in Harlem and in Detroit—disturbances which gave comfort and ammunition to America's enemies.

Alarmed and guilt-stricken, the Administration moved

swiftly to curtail these outbreaks. At first they felt that the suppression of the Negro press was in order; but common sense at last prevailed and concessions were made all along the line. A Negro general was named by Congress; a Negro fighter group was trained; Executive Order 8802 was issued; and in spots in the Army some Negroes were experimentally mixed with whites to die for a liberty they had never known.

During World War II, the Negro had, consciously or unconsciously, conducted himself abroad with admirable bearing. In France, Italy and England, the white masses were amazed at the US Negroes who, they had been taught to believe, were either frightened clowns or an unbelievable combination of child-beast whom one had either to take care of or to kill if he got out of hand. In England, public opinion was so strongly pro-Negro that many whites began to wonder at the restrained attitude of US Negroes. Intelligent English whites came to the conclusion that "these colored boys must have a deeply repressed life." There is a joke which tells more fully than social analysis the astonishment and liking which the English had for US Negroes. It is claimed that one night in a pub where several Negro GI's were drinking with their English friends an Englishman remarked: "I like you Americans a hell of a lot but I don't really care for those white people you brought over with you."

Negro jazz became the music for the proletarians of the cities of the world. In Paris, more experts exist on jazz than in the USA. The first critical books on jazz came from the pens of men like Hughes Panassié and others. Likewise, Negro literature, coming of age during the last days of the Depression and the beginning of the war, impressed the millions of European whites who then lived under the cruel domination of Hitler. Here, for the first time, the voice of the US Negro sounded a truly human and universal note which struck deep into the hearts of men living an existence full of pain and terror. The French *marquis* and the partisans of Italy read the novels of US Negroes, and for the first time they felt that here were people they understood; and they hoped that the Negroes could understand them. (My books, *Native Son* and *Black Boy* were first introduced into Europe in the undergrounds of France and Italy!) It was not difficult to convince the whites of Europe that American literature and Hollywood had smeared the Negro, for here was proof of a new kind of Negro and Europe liked him, for he spoke a language that these oppressed millions could understand. Indeed one could state an equation regarding the influence of the US Negro both on the musical and on the literary front in Europe. To the degree that millions of Europe's whites were terrorized and driven by Nazism, to that degree did they embrace the Negro's music and his literary expression. Here was a development that white America did not foresee or understand. Hence, the Negro became to a large measure for Europe the one and only human aspect of an otherwise brutally industrialized continent.

It took some time for the US to recognize that there actually existed a Cold War. It was at the London Conference of the Big Four that Secretary of State Marshall finally awoke and uttered his famous words to Molotov: "I don't believe that you believe what you are saying." The conference broke up and from that moment on the US whites knew that they were face to face with an implacable enemy who was aggressive on the cultural, economic, social and political fronts.

The US reaction was at first typically hesitant. A wave of self-consciousness entered the US. Then a feeling of guilt replaced self-consciousness as the US realized the full implication of Russia's Cold War. The USSR launched a wave of propaganda that literally held America and her pretensions and actions up to scorn throughout the world. America's only answer was to increase her own military might, which enabled the Russians to yell: "Look, America is preparing another war." Belatedly, the US saw that military might alone could not repel the Russian propaganda assault, that she had to try to either hide or correct those evils that Russia pointed out for other nations to look at.

So, for the second time within a decade, the US tried to address itself to its "Negro problem." Truman issued his order for the abolishment of Jim Crow in the armed services. He plugged for Civil Rights, etc. But not all of the US reactions to the Cold War were positive. Despite the fact that the US wanted to allay the Negro at home in order to take from Russia her propaganda weapon, the US sought to stifle expression at home by a wave of reaction against all liberal forces. Hence the rise of McCarthyism, etc. The US campaign was a delicate and dangerous thing, for while trying to mollify Negroes they still carried on their traditionally dangerous game of mob rule, mob reaction, mob feeling and mob security.

There were other factors, of course, in the nation's treatment of the Negro but this writer prefers to believe that the issue of the Cold War was decisive. There was the influence of the trade unions; there was the natural progress of the nation as a whole, which saw that nothing could be gained by oppressing Negroes. A white girl in North Carolina said to me once: "I don't see it. All the hanging and beating and killing of colored folks ain't gonna get us nothing at all." She was a poor white girl and to toss her the sop of being better than a Negro was not enough to satisfy her. But I have the conviction that all of these factors were not enough to turn the tide. It needed the overwhelming fear and threat and pressure of Russia's Cold War.

What was this threat, other than the embarrassment felt by the US in its propaganda war? It took a concrete turn in the minds of white Americans. They began to ask themselves just what would happen to the consciousness of the Negro whom they had kicked around for 300 years, if that Negro serving in a Jim Crow army should meet the Red Army in Czechoslovakia? And to ask such a question was to answer it. They knew. Hence, they rushed, with worry pushing them, to try to create a semblance of racial justice in the Army at least. And since they had to associate with Negroes, they felt that it was far better to associate with the ones who had been educated than with the ones who were raw and bitter about their oppression. Hence, white US had to reverse even their Deep South educational practices, in order to bridge the gap between Negroes and white America, a gap which their own policies had sought so hard with fire and murder to create and maintain. White hands, trembling with fear, hauled down for a few inches the standard of white supremacy!

For the US Negro, this situation is not as simple as it would seem at first sight. There are some fifteen million Negroes in the USA and to give a handful of them half of their rights in exchange for loyalty is to make the other millions wonder what will become of them. It also creates in the hearts of that handful a moral problem. In exchange for rights which are his by law ought a Negro cease making claims upon white America for the rights of his black brothers? Should a Negro consider himself as "bought" when he has received a big job? Should he hide the condition of his people before the bar of world public opinion in gratitude for what white US has given him? Or should he simply try to live as whites live and forget the "problem"? The answer to this question would be simple if US whites gave enough Negroes opportunity, that is, enough Negroes to constitute some kind of solid majority with material interests to defend. It must be recalled that, despite a few single gains, the vast majority of Negroes are downright poor, and when a minority of that group, having the talent and the duty to express themselves, decide to remain silent to protect their private holdings, then the rest of the Negroes are left defenseless. . . . That is the stark truth of the situation. Indeed, one could well contemplate a development of rigid class lines being drawn among Negroes on that basis.Already Negro spies are operating among Negroes, spying on Negroes for whites! This is the road to internecine racial bitterness among Negroes.

Another vital point must not be overlooked. Negroes who have arisen either through luck or talent to high international positions must realize that foreigners who meet and weigh them will do so in a broad human way. Ralph Bunche is not regarded fundamentally by Frenchmen as a Negro but as an American. They will watch him and judge him as an American. Will the future Bunches act like white Babbitts? If so, then the Negro stands to lose on the international scene much of that deep human sympathy he has so laboriously and at so great a cost built for himself. Above all, he, the Negro, must realize that he is not alone and cannot act and live alone in this world any more. He must realize that one of the things which has spurred white US to grant him a few concessions is the attitude of hostile criticism which foreign whites have held toward the US about her "Negro question." And there is no quicker way to make these foreign whites turn away from the Negro in disgust than to see our native blacks embracing the shallow materialistic values held by the dominant white majority. Many US Negroes serving abroad are being weighed and found wanting by white foreigners who have a deep sense of kinship with their plight. Just as the Negro has outgrown his spirituals, will he outgrow his fight for humanity? Will the Negro become just another American? If he does, he will have lost a great opportunity. . . .

Or can US Negroes, as they slowly come into their rights, be big enough men and women to try to help their country become a better country—a country which can compel not only the fear but the love and respect of the world, for today even America's allies fear and dread her. . . .

Abroad, in France and England, foreign whites who are not Communists, ask: "Why cannot the Negroes lead the US in a revolutionary movement for civil liberties? Why don't Negroes, seeing that their problem is a white problem, try to find allies among the whites and lead them to a broader and deeper conception of liberty and democracy?"

The US Negro should remark that his receiving a little more decent treatment is not occasioned by the Bill of Rights, the Constitution or the Declaration of Independence, but from fear of Russia! And he might well ask himself what will be his fate if and when the Cold War ends. Suppose the USSR were defeated? Would the USA continue to implement or try to implement her promises of justice to the Negro? The answer to this question will be found in observing how white US treated Negroes when there was no threat. It can be safely said that there will be a quick reversal. There will be an attempt to drive "the niggers back to their places." And there are plenty of poor whites willing and ready to help do it. Witness the recent Cicero incidents! The Negro, though enjoying some progress is still skating over thin ice.

It must not be naïvely assumed that the Negro will march

forward toward his rights without setbacks. These setbacks and advances will depend in a large measure upon the stresses and strains of US social and class relations and upon the tensions in the economic fabric. A Depression, a defeat in war, may cause rich US whites to rise and try to protect their society against the millions of poor whites who are clamoring to get their share. Why should not these rich whites pit poor whites against poor blacks? It has been successfully done in the past and can be done again. Such was Hitler's tactic, his Germany against the Jews, and we ought to recall that US Negroes do not in any way hold positions in the USA comparable to those held by Jews in Germany. It would be far easier for US whites to take the Negro as a scapegoat than it was for Germans to accept Jews as such.

> There is another book which should be taken off the book racks of the Nation; it should be removed from the bookstores; its sale should be stopped. It is the recent book of the month, which has had such a great sale. Senators can understand why it has had such a sale if they will read it. It is entitled "Black Boy," by Richard Wright. Richard Wright is a Mississippean. He was born and reared near Natchez, Miss. He went from Natchez to Jackson, from Jackson to Memphis, from Memphis to Chicago, and from Chicago to Brooklyn, N. Y., where he is married to a white woman and is living happily, he says. He wrote the book Black Boy ostensibly as the story of his life. Actually it is a damnable lie from beginning to end. It is practically all fiction. There is just enough truth to it to enable him to build his fabulous lies about his experiences in the South and his description of the people of the South and the culture, education, and life of Southern people. The purpose of the book is to plant the seeds of hate in every Negro in America against the white men of the South or against the white race anywhere, for that matter. That is the purpose. Its purpose is to plant the seeds of the devilment and troublebreeding in the days to come in the mind and heart of every American Negro. Read the book if you do not believe what I am telling you. It is the dirtiest, filthiest, lousiest, most obscene piece of writing that I have ever seen in print. I would hate to have a son or daughter of mine permitted to read it; it is so filthy and so dirty. But it comes from a Negro, and you cannot expect any better from a person of his type.
>
> —Senator Theodore Bilbo, June 25, 1945

Memphis and Chicago

Wright's Memphis

GRACE MCSPADDEN WHITE

Richard Wright spent two impressionable periods of his childhood and youth in Memphis, Tennessee. But today few Memphians know who Richard Wright is, and fewer still know that one of the great American writers not only lived in their city (though briefly, from 1925 to 1927), but that he wrote about Memphis and that his decision to become a writer was sharply influenced by an editorial he happened to read in the city's most respected newspaper.

Richard was about five years old when his family first moved to Memphis. He tells in *Black Boy* of the family's going on a boat to Memphis (p. 15; all page references here are to the Perennial Classics edition, Harper and Row, New York, 1966); he describes their living in a one-story tenement with concrete pavements and an absence of green, growing things. This period made two deep impressions on him: he "had had his first triumph over (his) father," (p. 18); and his father had deserted his mother and Richard's feelings about him were those of a stranger, speaking a different language (p. 42). The family left Memphis, without the father, when Richard was around seven years of age.

In *Black Boy* Wright describes a later meeting with his father upon the red clay of a Mississippi plantation; the meeting is poignant in its separation and misunderstanding. But there is an interesting foreshadowing of Wright's second Memphis period in the last lines of that account.

> From far beyond the horizons that bound this black plantation there had come to me through my living the knowl-

> edge that my father was a black peasant who had gone to the city seeking life, but who had failed in the city; a black peasant whose life had been hopelessly snarled in the city, and who had at last fled the city—that same city which had lifted me in its burning arms and borne me toward alien and undreamed-of-shores of knowing (p. 43; later page references are to *Black Boy*).

Although the young Richard could not have understood it at the time, there is adequate explanation for his father's life (and those of all Negroes) having been "hopelessly snarled in the city" in an editorial published in *The Memphis Daily Commercial,* on Sunday, October 18, 1890, just 18 years before Richard was born in 1908.

The editor is replying to a paper read by Dr. Mayo before the American Social Science Association. This "educator of high repute" states that the class known before the Civil War as "poor whites" is "coming to the front," and he concludes that "the Southern children on whom we are to largely depend thirty years hence for this glorious work of reconstruction and reconciliation are the rising Third Estate and the negroes, the youthful millions that now swarm this land of the South."

Disagreeing sharply with Dr. Mayo, the editor states:

> There are but two estates—the white and the black. Race makes and marks the dividing line, and this must always be the case so long as the superior stands in presence of the inferior race. There is a law of being, of existence, of blood, superior to all written law, which impels the whites to this position. . . . The Celto-Teutonic races have only a faint toleration for what they consider and experience and history proves to be inferior races, with which they cannot live on terms of equality, and which they cannot assimilate and absorb by marriage. . . . The race feeling is with the people and not the suppositious leaders whom Dr. Mayo (and others) have in their minds. It is the instinct of development of the survival of the fittest by the process of natural selection which history exemplifies in the progress of the English and all the Continental Europeans.

Mr. Fred L. Hutchins, a letter carrier in Memphis for nearly 45 years, recounted many incidents that illustrate the social situation and racial climate in Memphis during the Wrights' first period there. Although he did not know Richard Wright himself, Mr. Hutchins is a recognized authority on Beale Street and on Negroes and Negro life. His family moved to Memphis from Mississippi in 1888. "Less than two weeks later," he states, "a riot was started at the 'Curve.' At that time they called Walker Avenue and Mississippi the 'Curve,' taking its name from the street car rails curving off Mississippi onto Walker. Three young Negro men had a grocery store on that corner, and a white man ran one on the opposite corner. Trouble started when whites threw rocks into the colored store and then fired pistols. The colored men returned the fire and two deputies were hit.

"The three men who ran this store were Thomas Moss, Will Steward and Calvin McDowell. Tom Moss was not in the store when this trouble started, but was at home. McDowell was arrested with Will Steward. Then they went to Tom Moss's home and picked him up and put all three in jail. Four or five days later, they took them out and lynched the three. Moss knew nothing of the trouble, but was compelled to share the fate of the other two. As a result of the lynching, many Negroes became upset and left Memphis, going to Oklahoma. Just three years before that, President Harrison had issued a proclamation opening the much-sought lands of Oklahoma to settlers."

"Years ago," Mr. Hutchins continues, "when a white man saw a policeman he felt safe. When a Negro saw a policeman, he left. One Sunday at Main and Madison, a white man saw a colored man go by wearing a straw hat. The white knocked the colored's straw hat off his head and jumped on it, crushing it. A policeman was standing right there and when the Negro protested to the police, he said, 'Get away from here, Nigger, don't try to start something. You know you can't whip all these white men around here.' "

Mr. Hutchins ends on a hopeful note, which he reiterated both in conversations and in letters. "I have seen just about a little of everything in Memphis, but now Memphis has changed to a better city. There is not as much prejudice now. If the colored people will take care of themselves and overcome the lack of cultural and educational opportunities, there is hope for us all. Within the last eight or ten years, things have been better."

Richard Wright's second period in Memphis began with the hope that he was headed to "a land where I could live with a little less fear" (p. 227). He arrived in Memphis on "a cold November Sunday morning in 1925, seventeen years of age." He headed immediately toward the famous Beale Street he had heard "was filled with danger: pickpockets, prostitutes, cutthroats, and black confidence men." He rented a room in a house listed as 570 Beale Avenue in the Memphis City Directory. Of this first experience in the big city on the notorious Beale Street, he comments after having experienced the kindness and warmth of his landlady: "It was on reputedly disreputable Beale Street in Memphis that I had met the warmest, friendliest person I had ever known, that I discovered that all human beings were not mean and driving, were not bigots like the members of my family" (p. 230).

His first act was to find a job. He walked down Beale Street and into the heart of Memphis. "While wandering aimlessly about the streets of Memphis, gaping at the tall buildings and the crowds, killing time, eating bags of popcorn, I was struck by an odd sudden idea. If I had attempted to work for an optical company in Jackson and had failed, why should I not try to work for an optical company in Memphis" (p. 244).

This sudden decision changed the direction of his life. He found the Merry Optical Company (in 1922 changed to the American Optical Company), took the elevator to the fifth floor, and was interviewed by a white man. He was quite open and honest about why he had been fired from the Jackson company and told the man he wanted a chance to learn the optical trade. "That's not our policy," the white man said, but he hired Richard at eight dollars per week and a promised raise of a dollar a week until he was receiving ten. Wright wrote, "I accepted it. I liked the open, honest way in which the man talked to me; and, too, the place seemed clean, brisk, businesslike" (p. 245).

One of the exciting discoveries I made in my attempt to

retrace Wright's second Memphis period was to talk with two men who had worked with him in the American Optical Company and who remembered him. Mr. Edwin E. Shroyer, Sr. was superintendent of production of the operation. It was then located on the 5th, 6th, and 7th floors of the American Bank Building at 144 Madison, the site now occupied by the Manhattan Branch of the Union Planters National Bank. Mr. Shroyer was with the company until his retirement in 1942: he is now 79 years of age.

When asked what he remembered about the young man from Mississippi, Mr. Shroyer said, "He was an errand boy who did his work well for a colored boy. He had a good disposition and was nice looking." Then he qualified this with the phrase often used in the early 1900's, "as long as he stayed in his place."

"I remember that he used to read a lot," he continued, "particularly the *Argosy* magazine and a lot of books. I know that he did some writing while he was working at the optical company and I read a very short part of one of the first things he wrote." He also spoke of another messenger named Allan Dupree and mentioned that he was literary, too; that he and Wright were friends, and that he remembered Dupree as always laughing.

"When he left the company and went to Chicago, he wrote his book, *Native Son,*" Mr. Shroyer said. "I got the book but read little of it. I always enjoyed reading, but this book did not appeal to me."

The other employee I talked with did not wish to be identified by name; but he, too, remembered Richard Wright and spoke very highly of his work. A laboratory technician, this man probably had more frequent contact with Wright, since Wright speaks of his work as that of being "assigned to run errands and wash eyeglasses after they had come from the rouge-smeared machines. Each evening I had to take sacks of packages to the post office for mailing. It was light work and I was fast on my feet" (p. 245). The laboratory technician described him as "honest, good, that he attended to his own business and was a credit to the company." He also knew Allan

Dupree and stated that both errand boys were ambitious. He remembered that Richard Wright left the company soon after the fall of 1927.

Both these men and others to whom I talked gave me names of porters who worked in the building and who probably knew Richard Wright, but I have been unable to locate any of them. In *Black Boy* Wright names several other Negroes who worked in the building: "an old man whom we called Edison; his son, John, and a night janitor who answered to the name of Dave" (p. 250). One of the people I talked with thought that "John" was really Allan Dupree, but there was no way to trace this speculation, since Dupree died several years ago. It is also possible that the night watchman called "Spank" in *Black Boy* is a man listed in the current Memphis Telephone Directory as Sanverneado Crawford, at 2461 Brooklyn. But telephone and letter attempts to contact him were unanswered.

I went to Beale Street to try to locate Wright's residence. But nobody in the general area remembered anything about the rooming house or about the young errand boy. Despite the fact that the actual time Wright spent in Memphis was from November, 1926, to the winter of 1927, Wright is listed in Memphis City Directories as living at three different addresses:

(1926) Wright, Rich'd, msngr, Am. Optical Co., 570 Beale Avenue.

(1927) Wright, Richard N, msngr, Am. Optical Co., 875 Griffith Pl.

(1928) Wright, Richard, msngr, Am. Optical Co., 370 Washington.

The manager of a liquor store on the corner of Beale and Washington introduced me to Mr. Ray Williams, now 72 years of age, who said he knew Richard Wright in connection with a pharmacy named Batte's, operated by the Martin Brothers, well-known Memphis doctors and dentists. He said that Wright was frequently in this store, which was a favorite hang-out for the area. This was in the days of Prohibition, and since by his own statement Mr. Williams was a successful bootlegger, he had many opportunities to know the people on Beale Street! He revealed this fact with a wonderful grin and a measure of pride. He said that Richard Wright lived with Jed W. Martin, but which residence this was, he did not know. Williams later became a pullman porter and was on the Memphis-Chicago run. "I ran into Richard Wright several times in Chicago," he said. "He was a beautiful character and his conduct was of the highest quality."

While the routine life of the city went on around him, Richard Wright was patronizing secondhand bookstores, buying magazines and books. "In this way I became acquainted with periodicals like *Harper's, The Atlantic Monthly*, and the *American Mercury*. I would buy them for a few cents, read them, then resell them to the bookdealer" (p. 248).

The zest for learning eventually led to the most important decision in Wright's life. "Though I did not have to report for work until nine o'clock each morning, I would arrive at eight and go into the lobby of the downstairs bank—where I knew the Negro porter—and read the early edition of the Memphis *Commercial Appeal,* thereby saving myself five cents each day, which I spent for lunch" (p. 248). One morning he picked up the paper as usual and began his free reading. "I came finally to the editorial page and saw an article dealing with one H. L. Mencken. I knew by hearsay that he was the editor of the *American Mercury*, but aside from that I knew nothing about him. The article was a furious denunciation of Mencken, concluding with one, hot, short sentence: Mencken is a fool" (p. 267).

The effect on Wright was bewildering. "The only people I had heard denounced in the South were the Negroes, and this man was not a Negro. Then what ideas did Mencken hold that made a newspaper like the *Commercial Appeal* castigate him publicly? Undoubtedly he must be advocating ideas that the South did not like. Were there, then, people other than Negroes who criticized the South?" (p. 267).

He immediately set out to find out who this Mencken

was. Not far from the optical company was the large Cossitt Library. Negroes were not allowed to use the library, but Wright decided that there was one man, an Irish Catholic, who might lend him his card because he, too, seemed to be hated by the white Southerners who called him a "Pope lover." Although the man is not named, he was probably Joseph Beeker, but I could find no trace of him today. The man allowed Wright to use his library card.

Wright forged a note which said: "Dear Madam: Will you please let this nigger boy—I used the word 'nigger' to make the librarian feel that I could not possibly be the author of the note—have some books by H. L. Mencken?" Then he signed the white man's name. On the first occasion at the library he had a moment of fear when the librarian wanted to know what books by Mencken were wanted, and then asked, "You're not using these books are you?" Wright suggested that she call the man, and the danger passed. The librarian gave him two books. A block away from the library, he opened one of them and read the title: *A Book of Prefaces.* "I was nearing my nineteenth birthday and I did not know how to pronounce the word 'preface,'" Wright wrote. He looked at the other book called *Prejudices.* "I knew what that word meant; I had heard it all my life" (p. 271).

In connection with this incident, statements by Miss Mary DeVant, who worked for years in the Memphis Historical Section of the Cossitt Library, are illuminating. Now retired but interested in Memphis history, she said she did not begin working at Cossitt until June, 1928, and that the librarian who gave the books to Wright was now living in Columbia, Missouri. Miss DeVant said that maids and other messengers frequently took out books from Cossitt, and that the staff suspected they might themselves be reading the books, but that nothing was said about it unless there was some reason to suspect that the cards had been lost or stolen. The official policy of the library was to refer Negroes to the library at LeMoyne College, a Negro school. This may have been in the mind of the librarian who asked Wright if he was planning to read the books himself.

On this significant occasion Richard Wright went to his room after work and read the Mencken books. "I was jarred and shocked by the style, the clear, clean, sweeping sentences. Why did he write like that? And how did one write like that? . . . Yes, this man was fighting, fighting with words. He was using words as a weapon, using them as one would use a club. Could words be weapons? No. It frightened me. I read on and what amazed me was not what he said, but how on earth anybody had the courage to say it" (p. 272). Wright read all the books and authors Mencken talked about, and became aware that the impulse to dream had been slowly beaten out of him by experience. It was surging up again, and he hungered for new ways of looking at things, of "being affected by something that made the look of the world different" (p. 273).

The world became different indeed for him. He now knew what being a Negro meant. "I could endure the hunger. I had learned to live with hate. But to feel that there were feelings denied me, that the very breath of life itself was beyond my reach, that more than anything else hurt, wounded me. I had a new hunger" (p. 274).

While Wright was there, Memphis had not been aware that a writer destined for greatness was being affected by its people and customs and attitudes. But in later years Memphians had occasion to take note of him and of his relationships to the city. On March 10, 1940, the *Memphis Commercial Appeal* carried a favorable review of Wright's *Native Son,* written by Jack Lockhart. And in the book review page of the same newspaper, dated April 22, 1940, *Native Son* is listed as second on the Best Selling Book List of Fiction. The review of *Black Boy* in *The Commercial Appeal* of April 1, 1945, represents an openly-stated attempt by a Southern reviewer with "a fair share of prejudice" to strive for "objectivity and strict justice." Even before this review appeared, the large downtown Goldsmith's department store was advertising *Black Boy* amongst "Three New Books of the World Today"—and touting Wright as "the author of *Native Son,* that reached such popularity some time ago."

A book published in 1948 concerning Memphis calls specific attention to Wright's work and the racial situation reflected in his books. Shields McIlwaine gives a section in his *Memphis Down in Dixie* to "What Negroes Mean to Memphis." He writes:

> Of course, every day in downtown Memphis, most white men meet, talk, and transact some small business with Negroes—stock clerks, messengers, delivery boys, bootblacks, elevator operators, and pencil-selling or singing beggars. Many of these black men have served in certain buildings for a long time and enjoy the friendliness, tolerance, and kindness of the traditional Southern way with colored personal servants. Certainly few Negroes downtown ever suffered the sadism or spent their waking hours seething like Richard Wright. In the Memphis climate, people, white or black, don't have the spare energy for hating around the clock as some readers might infer from Wright's *Black Boy.* Yet, by and large, the relation between white and black men downtown is not close when compared with the daylong intimacy of the housewife and her 'good girl.' (Dutton and Co., New York, p. 316.)

Since that book was published in 1948, significant changes have occurred in racial attitudes and practices in Memphis, but not without resistance. In June, 1957, a move was made to integrate the Memphis Public Library. Jesse H. Turner applied for permission to borrow books from the library both for himself and for his children: a resident of Memphis since his discharge as a captain from the armed forces in 1946, Mr. Turner had previously attended LeMoyne College and the University of Chicago and was a graduate of each of these institutions.

In August, 1958, Mr. Turner filed suit in Federal Court asking that "negroes" be permitted to use all public library facilities in Memphis. Four members of the City Commission strongly opposed integration and said, "We will fight any lawsuit that seeks to force it." Those members included Henry Loeb, present Memphis mayor, the man who was at the center of the controversies concerning the garbage workers' protest at the time Martin Luther King was assassinated in Memphis.

In March, 1960, demonstrations and sit-ins supporting the pending Jesse Turner suit were organized by students from LeMoyne College and Owen College and by the Memphis

Branch of the NAACP. Massive arrests for "loitering" and "disturbing the peace" and "creating a public nuisance" followed; five reporters from two Negro newspapers were amongst those arrested. In various pulpits Negro ministers were urging their congregations to attend the trials of those arrested. In a court hearing in March, 1960, in connection with these mass arrests, City Judge Beverly Boushe declared:

> This situation (segregation) has been in existence for more than 200 years. It is not only the custom, it is the law. . . . We are not trying the question of civil rights or segregation or integration here today. . . . The sole question with which this court is concerned here today is that of maintaining the peace and dignity of the community. (Memphis *Commercial Appeal,* March 22, 1960.)

The Reverend Ben Hooks, the black lawyer defending the demonstrators, told Judge Boushe that "no amount of fines will stop occurrences such as this one." He continued: "We are living in a transitory age. Customs are being abandoned. We have tried to work with the white community, but the white community takes the position that 'we are not going to move.' "

Finally, after weeks of public distress and behind-the-scenes discussions and before a court order requiring it was handed down, the seven branches of the Memphis Public Library discontinued their policy of segregation. On October 13, 1960 the City Commission announced: "The City Commission has decided the facilities of the public libraries shall be made available to all the citizens of the city." *(Memphis Commercial Appeal,* October 14, 1960.)

It is somehow strangely appropriate that the Memphis Public Libraries were desegregated just one month before Richard Wright died in Paris on November 30, 1960. Each date marks the passing of an era. When I was in Memphis doing this research, Judge Beverly Boushe's death was announced on August 29, 1971. There are ironies in human life. I was interested to see that the obituary for Judge Bousche made no mention of his part in the significant library integration case. Richard Wright's death was noted in both the *Memphis Commercial Appeal* and the *Memphis Press-Scimitar*, although neither carried a picture nor made much of his having lived in Memphis.

In Memphis today there are remarkable signs of change, in concrete achievement and in future plans. But some things do not change; they yield reluctantly if at all. The city is restoring Wright's Beale Street. According to Charles E. Dille III, an architectural planner, the intention in restoring Beale Street is "to create a vital entertainment strip, combining the colorful musical heritage of W. C. Handy's era with the very active and unique Memphis sound and the present-day music industry that have made our city the nation's fourth-ranking recording center." When asked if anything commemorative was planned for Richard Wright, Mr. Dille replied that he did not know who Richard Wright was.

But whether Memphis feels Wright's presence, there is no doubt that Memphis was always present to him. In a letter to his friend Joe C. Brown, Wright wrote from Chicago on March 5, 1938, "The folks I write about live in Chicago, in Memphis, and down there in old Mississippi." When he headed north, Wright carried with him roots deeply nurtured in Delta soil. However limiting and hostile that nurture had been, because he felt deeply enough and was conscious of his own possibilities, he was "full of a hazy notion that life could be lived with dignity, that the personalities of others could not be violated, that men should be able to confront other men without fear or shame, and that if men were lucky in their living on earth they might win some redeeming meaning for their having struggled and suffered here beneath the stars" (p. 285).

* * *

In addition to those persons mentioned in the text, I owe deep and particular thanks to the following people who helped in the preparation of this study: my daughter-in-law, Susan Stone Overholser of Nashville; Mary Pennell Simonton Boothe of Memphis; Dewey Pruett, Curator, The Mississippi Valley Collection of the John Willard Brister Library, Memphis State University; Nat Jorel of the Memphis Public Library and Information Center; my husband, W. D. White, Professor of English and Religion at St. Andrews College.

A Reminiscence

JACK CONROY

I first saw Richard Wright several months after I had published one of his poems in *The Anvil,* which I was then editing at Moberly, Missouri. The occasion was a John Reed Club convention in Chicago to which came writers (published and unpublished) and artists (hung and unhung) from all over the Midwest. They got there by whatever means they could manage. Some arrived as free riding passengers on freight trains, some were experimenting with the then unusual method of hitch-hiking, others had pooled their pennies to buy gas for asthmatic Fords. A few were rich enough to arrive luxuriantly by passenger train ("on the cushions" it was called) or by a cheaper (but fancy for most of us) bus.

My young niece's "feller" (as boy friends were called in Moberly) had a fairly dependable Model A Ford and was willing to travel if somebody would cough up for the gas. Two young sprouts, honing for a taste of city pleasures, joined me in scraping up the wherewithal and we made it to the great city by the big lake. We even had enough to spend a night in a State Street "hotel" (not a flop house, in which everybody sleeps in the same room) where for a quarter you got a plasterboard cubicle just big enough for a one-man cot. Chickenwire was stretched across the top which gave a measure of privacy, but didn't keep out sounds or smells. The cubicles were built in a lofty room that once had accommodated a factory. The gurgles, d.t. ravings and odoriferous exhalations from fore and aft of the other guests kept the Moberly boys awake, but not me. I had been through it all before.

There was a black and tan burlesque show hard by with well-stacked Negro and white girls dexterously bumping and grinding in separate but equal formations. A kind of segregation prevailed, as white girls and black girls never danced together. The comedians and straight men were white. These and other cultural divertissements beguiled my travelling companions while I repaired to the upstairs headquarters of the John Reed Club, just down the street. An only slightly sour hot dog with last week's bun and plenty of mustard could be had for a nickel on the downstairs level; two bits would buy you a rather substantial, though somewhat greasy, meal.

The John Reed Club convention was a fine experience; spiritually my sad sick heart had long languished in the alien corn of Moberly. It was a time when we kept in touch with long letters (an art which seems largely lost nowadays) but print is a poor substitute for pressing the friendly flesh now and then.

One of my *Anvil* contributors (who prudently wrote under a pseudonym out of deference for his superiors at the post office where he was a mail sorter) had told me of a young Negro fellow worker who cherished literary ambitions and was "pretty good." This turned out to be Richard Wright, and I referred both of them to the John Reed Club. "I don't think either of us will ever regret it," my contributor told me. I don't think Wright did. His talents seemed to proliferate in those early days in the John Reed Club; he wrote with more confidence. Much of his disillusionment with the left-wing movement stemmed from his dismay at the arbitrary ukase of the C. P. dissolving the John Reed Clubs.

Sam Gaspar, an Armenian-American who liked to call himself "the poor man's Saroyan," was an established member of what came to be known as the Chicago post office school of writers. He was a contributor to *The Anvil* and other "little" magazines. Sam died last year, still full of piss and vinegar with his big white teeth flashing as we talked of the old days about six weeks before his death. Like many another of our group, he never had a book published but was still striving and hoping for one when the final darkness fell. In the basement across the street from club headquarters, Sears was dispensing generous free samples of what seemed to us a very palatable California wine (a dollar a gallon if you had a dollar to spare, which we didn't). Sam and I doubled up in the line several times till the busy dispenser started giving us a hard look. We thought of a disguise like a false mustache, but by that time were a bit elevated anyhow. I had seen Dick Wright earlier, but he had vanished from the convention hall. I encountered him later in the evening at an apartment party where he sat alone, a good-looking and pleasant-mannered young man but abstracted and aloof from the alcoholically induced merriment about him. In all the times I saw him, he seldom drank at all and if so sparingly and with no visible effect. Childhood memories about drunkenness must have lingered.

When I landed in Chicago in 1938 to work on the Illinois Writers' Project and to join with Nelson Algren in establishing *The New Anvil,* Dick had departed for New York for a job on the project there and also to moonlight as Harlem correspondent of *The Daily Worker.* He frequently returned to Chicago, however, always inquiring, taking notes, buttonholing Negroes on the South Side and as often as not repelling and frightening them by his persistent inquisitiveness. Nelson Algren was living in an arcade flanked by storefronts jerrybuilt to accommodate enterprises connected with the World's Columbian Exposition of 1893. Algren's studio was in one of these storefronts, and as he, Dick and I sat one morning drinking coffee, the Negro janitor for the buildings appeared with brush and broom. Dick was then working on an article about the policy racket in Chicago, and Nelson knew that the janitor played it regularly (a nickel or a dime holding out the promise of a vast haul) and had recently won a small sum. Despite Nelson's assurance that Dick was "all right," the janitor buttoned his lip about policy. He later said he was sure the persistent, smooth-talking stranger was "a law man or something" and hence not to be trusted.

Again, a group of us were whooping it up in a small Negro joint called the "Five Spot" just across the line on Cottage Grove Avenue, which still more or less divided the Negro ghetto from the down-at-the-heels mansions of the long-since-fled white aristocrats. Dick began to quiz some of the habitués, and as usual got the fish eye. Not from one, though. This one surmised from his good clothes and fluent talk that Dick was the representative of a fraternal society to which he belonged and thus was obligated to treat him with some deference. Muttering some cabalistic password, he attempted to shake hands with Dick—to cement their common bond by bestowing the secret grip known only to initiates. His protestations and denials unheeded, Dick fled in disgust. The lodge brother upbraided his retreating form for ingratitude and snootishness. Hadn't he paid good dues into the lodge for Dick's enjoyment, and wasn't he going to think twice before he shelled out any more?

During another visit Dick was telling me about his first plane trip, from New York to Chicago. As the plane left the ground, he said, he was swept by some sort of unreasoning terror.

"Did you ever smell your blood?" he asked.

"Can't say that I did," I answered.

"I did. I smelt my own blood."

This episode took on new meaning when I read in Horace Cayton's autobiography *Long Old Road* about a trip he and Dick took to Fisk University, where Horace had been addressing a seminar on race relations and Dick had spoken before a general assembly of students. The University, cognizant of the Jim Crow rules still in effect on the railroads, had booked them a compartment for the trip down South. Due to a mixup, they had to take a section on the way back. Dick won the toss for the lower berth. Horace, climbing down in the night, saw that the light was still on in Dick's berth. Parting the curtain, he beheld Dick fully clothed and sleepless. When Horace asked him how come, he answered:

"When I'm down South I want steel between me and those white folks, not just a cloth curtain."

Though he didn't say so then, I have since wondered after reading Cayton's story if the close proximity of white folks all around him in the close confines of the plane cabin might not have caused the terror that led him to fancy that he had smelled his own blood.

Richard Wright and the Communist Party

DANIEL AARON

In 1920, H. L. Mencken reviewed for *Smart Set* Mary White Ovington's *The Shadow,* a "bad novel" which the pundit used as an object lesson for Black writers. After summarizing its improbable plot and commenting on the superiority of Black music to Black literature (largely polemics and lyrical verse), he advised Miss Ovington "to forget her race prejudices and her infantile fables long enough to get a true and unemotional and typical picture of her people on paper." Only then would she "achieve a respectable work of art" and serve the cause she believed in.

The fact that Mary White Ovington was not black undermined Mencken's injunction, but it did not invalidate a remarkable statement in which he defined the as yet unwritten great Black novel and its Negro author.

> The black man, I suppose, has a fairly good working understanding of the white man; he has many opportunities to observe and note down, and my experience of him convinces me that he is a shrewd observer—that few white men ever fool him. But the white man, even in the South, knows next to nothing of the inner life of the negro. The more magnificently he generalizes, the more his ignorance is displayed. What the average Southerner believes about the Negroes who surround him is chiefly nonsense. His view of them is moral and indignant or, worse still, sentimental and idiotic. The great movements and aspirations that stir them are quite beyond his comprehension; in many cases he does not even hear of them. The thing we need is a realistic picture of this inner life of the Negro by one who sees the race from within—a self portrait as vivid and accurate as Dostoievsky's por-

> trait of the Russian or Thackeray's of the Englishman. The action should be kept within the normal range of Negro experience. It should extend over a long enough range of years to show some development in character and circumstance. It should be presented against a background made vivid by innumerable small details. The Negro author who makes such a book will dignify American literature and accomplish more for his race than a thousand propagandists and theorists. He will force the understanding that now seems so hopeless. He will blow up nine-tenths of the current poppycock.

This literary redeemer, Mencken warned, would have to take care to avoid the wrong literary models: "The place to learn how to write novels is in the harsh but distinguished seminary kept by Prof. Dr. Dreiser."

Some half-dozen years later, Richard Wright, a young black man who would ultimately fill these specifications, discovered the *Prefaces* of Mencken in the Memphis public library. Mencken, who had probably insulted the South more flagrantly and vehemently and colorfully than any other American writer, was subject to editorial attacks in all of the Southern newspapers at that time. Here was a rambunctious man striking out at everything sacred to Americans—political, social, religious—and "fighting with words . . . using words as weapons . . . using them as one would a club." The self-taught boy who had just managed to finish eighth grade learned from Mencken the names of writers he would soon read: Poe, Conrad, France, Dostoievsky, Mark Twain, Anderson, Lewis—and above all, Dreiser. "All my life," Wright wrote later, "had shaped me for the realism, the naturalism of the modern novel, and I could not read enough of them." It excited him to think that men all over the world were fighting against oppression—that he wasn't alone in his rebellion. The discovery of Mencken encouraged him to become a writer, and the reading of the realists mentioned by Mencken pointed Wright in the direction of Communism.

Wright's account of his arrival in Chicago in 1927 resembles the experiences of other men and women in real life or in literature who come to the Big City from the provinces.

One thinks for example of the heroine of Dreiser's *Sister Carrie* (a novel Wright read with deep interest) or the hero of *An American Tragedy.* Chicago wasn't a vision out of the "Arabian Nights" as it was to Clyde Griffith, but it was exciting and frightening enough. Wright was astonished at first by the indifference of the white Chicagoan to the black newcomers, but in time he saw that his people had only exchanged masters—the Bosses of the Buildings for the Lords of the Land.

Wright described the impact of Chicago very eloquently in "How Bigger Was Born," and later he speculated on the gains and losses attending the black migration from the rural South to the Northern cities. Observing the misery of the urban black, the white man might wonder why the Negro had abandoned his Southern shack for an urban slum. Wright likened the black migration to the white man's breaking out of the "slumberous feudal world" to take the risks of what William James called "unguaranteed existence." In leaving the South, the Negro acted on "the same impulses" that motivated the white western activists who left the known for the unknown. He shared the hopes as well as the corruptions and psychological maladies of white men, but in the "cold industrial North," there existed a "saving remnant of a passion for freedom," and that was worth a good deal to Richard Wright with his secret ambitions.

So we find Wright in the Chicago of the late 1920's leading two lives simultaneously—one literary and intellectual, the other social. In a flat running with cockroaches, he read Stephen Crane and Dostoievsky and Gertrude Stein's *Three Lives* (a book that struck him as forcibly as it had Sherwood Anderson). His chief problem, with the advent of the Depression, was not in finding enough books to read but in finding jobs—or rather holding on to them. Thousands of other boys and young men went through similar experiences during the Thirties. They worked as porters, bill collectors, dish-washers, hospital orderlies, postoffice workers, counsellors (these were some of the jobs Wright had); but few listened so attentively to the jive talk of the urban blacks, observed the behavior at rent parties, or watched the expressions on the faces of unemployed men and women as they resisted evictions or stood up to the police.

Wright described his attitude at this time (between 1927 and 1931) as one of "watchful wonder," and his desire increased "to measure accurately the reality of the objective world so that I might more than meet its demands." He was old enough and mature enough to record the Depression and to respond to events that practically determined he would become a writer. The fat years for the Chicago blacks—which began in 1924—came to an end in 1929; they felt the onset of the long slide downward at least a year before white Chicagoans discerned the full impact of the economic collapse. Negro-owned banks were the first to fail, black workers the first to be fired. By 1932, the Black Belt was in the depths of deprivation. In and out of jobs during this period, Wright watched the relief kitchens being set up, watched middle-class relief officials interviewing their unemployed clients, saw how quickly the inchoate and confused mass of people developed feelings of solidarity as they anxiously waited in the employment offices or helped one another in the streets. "I was slowly beginning," Wright recalled, "to comprehend the meaning of my environment; a sense of direction was beginning to emerge from the conditions of my life. I began to feel something more powerful than I could express. My speech and manner changed. My cynicism slid from me. I grew open and questioning. I wanted to know."

And then one of those events occurred that have a kind of Horatio Algerish significance. A case worker assigned to the Wright household discovered Richard Wright. This chance meeting with the wife of a Chicago sociologist, Louis Wirth, brought Wright to the University where he met Wirth—and, more important, Wirth's assistant, Horace Cayton—a black intellectual who had arrived in the Black Metropolis via the Northwest and who was to become one of Wright's closest friends.

Cayton, in his autobiography, *Long Old Road* (1963), tells about his friendship with Wright and how the massive sociological data gathered by the Chicago sociologists helped to provide the ballast for *Native Son.* It was somehow appropriate that Wright should write the introduction to St. Clair Drake's and Cayton's impressive study of Chicago Negroes, *Black Metropolis,* for he was doing something equivalent in his fiction. This is not to say that he would not have written his books without the assistance of the Chicago school. There were other goads, as we shall see, to his imagination.

The story of Wright's connection with the actual or would-be Communist world in the early Thirties is familiar to anyone who has read his autobiographical writings. In 1932, he became involved with the Chicago John Reed Club, an organization sponsored by the Communist Party in 1929 to co-ordinate the activities of radical artists and writers. Wright had heard Communists haranguing crowds in Washington Park, but it was not until a white social worker invited him to a meeting that he came to know any of them. Suspicious at first he soon warmed up to people who, he felt, regarded him as a person only incidentally black. The Marxist literature they gave him to read demonstrated to him that the black downtrodden formed only a portion of the oppressed toilers. Some of the artists he met at the Club were to become as famous as himself—men like Nelson Algren, Jackson Pollock, Ben Shahn. Most of the members were simply young people looking for cultural stimulation. In this sympathetic environment Wright began gradually to find his own voice amidst the rhetoric and clichés of revolution. Not surprisingly, he joined the Party.

Wright's autobiographical remarks on the John Reed Club of Chicago and his subsequent dealings with the League of American Writers are all tinted a little, but essentially his account is reliable and only suffers from revealing omissions. The first national conference of the John Reed Clubs met in Chicago, May 29, 1932. The unpublished minutes of that Conference both complement and qualify Wright's recollections of the internal schisms and factional fights within the Chicago John Reed Club.

The temporary chairman of the Conference was the same Jan Wittenber who served as the model for Jan Erlone in

Native Son. (It was through him that Wright had joined the John Reed Club in January, 1932). Wittenber, a member of the artists' faction of the CP, sided with those John Reed members who preferred to entrust all questions of politics to the "militant leadership of the Communist Party." His description of the Club's activities show the kinds of work other members of the John Reed Club (and presumably Richard Wright) were engaged in that year.

However, his almost poignant summary of purposeful activity makes no mention of reaching out to the Negro masses, nothing about bringing in young proletarian writers like Richard Wright. The 1932 Conference boiled down to such questions as the proper approach to fellow-traveling intellectuals like John Dos Passos or Edmund Wilson, or debates on the danger of left sectarianism as against a too latitudinarian approach to writers and politics. Most interesting and portentous, the minutes indicate implicitly if not explicitly that individualists in the local clubs already distrusted the Central Party and the New York writers in particular, high-powered intellectuals from the East, who dominated the Conference. Clearly, even in 1932, the CP ran the show; and clearly the New York contingent wanted to exclude the inexperienced and uninfluential 'boys' (as Mike Gold called them) and to make the John Reed Clubs attractive to big names. As Wright knew well, the reconstitution of the Clubs did not take into consideration the needs and interests of Black artists.

Until the late Twenties, the 'Negro Question' for the Party was primarily a political and economic one—that is, until Stalin initiated the principle of a separate black nation in the United States. Of course, the Party line vacillated. The policy of Black self-determination, maintained between 1928 and 1934, was played down during the Popular Front period (1934-1939) only to be revived briefly following the Nazi-Soviet Pact. After Hitler invaded the USSR, the Party line switched again. At no time during these years, however, did the Party exercise much influence on the majority of American Blacks. When Wright joined the CP, it numbered about 16,000, of which barely more than a thousand were Negroes.

Some Black Communists considered the notion of a separate Black state within the United States highly unrealistic, as well as smacking of a kind of Red Jim Crowism. All Party people agreed, however, that the Party had failed to reach the Black proletariat and that Negro artists were partly to blame. As one Black leader put it in 1928:

> There is little in recent Negro poetry that would lead one to believe that the poets are conscious of the existence of the Negro masses. There is no challenge in their poetry, no revolt. They do not echo the lamentations of the downtrodden masses. Millions of blacks are suffering from poverty and cruelty, and the black poets shut their eyes! There is not a race more desperate in this country than the black race, and Negro poets play with pale emotions!

He added that most Negro writers were simply petit-bourgeois opportunists or black decadents or cowards.

This animus lay behind the Party's attempt to recruit Black writers who would inject Marxist militancy into black writing and give the lie to those who played the role of the "Meek Moses" and "Black Hamlet"—who shunned protest and refused to confront the revolutionary traditions of the Negro people. So it was that in 1932-1933, when Wright was working with the John Reed Club in Chicago, the Party singled him out as the type of proletarian revolutionary artist—free of the bourgeois taint—it had been seeking. Here was some one who could "eradicate the distorted stereotypes of the Negro people prevalent in American literature and drama" and write about the struggle of the masses. To the Party at this time, middle-class intellectuals like Walter White and W. E. B. DuBois were traitors. It looked to writers like Wright to lead Black America's fight against the "foes of culture and progress."

Wright was very receptive to this appeal in 1932—and with good reasons. He saw Communists not only fighting for Negro rights but also seeking to uproot racism within their own ranks. They pushed Blacks into Party work (Wright was elected President of the John Reed Club without his knowing why); they nominated Negroes for political office, dramatized the Black man's problem, risked social ostracism and even physical violence in behalf of Black people. No political party since the Abolitionists challenged American racial hypocrisy so zealously.

Wright's explanation of why he left the Party makes it abundantly clear at the same time why it had such a hold on him when he joined it and why he remained a radical after he left the Party in the early Forties. He says (and this is probably true, although how conscious he was of this reason it is hard to say) that as early as 1932 he felt the Party oversimplified Black experience. But the Party *had* a program, an ideal, and he, Richard Wright (this was his function as he saw it then) would tell the Communists how the common people felt. He would also tell the Black masses of the sacrifices the Communists were making for them. What notions Wright held about the Black Republic at this time is hard to say, but the white Jewish lawyer's description of American Blacks in *Native Son* may suggest a clue: "They are not simply twelve million people; in reality, they constitute a separate nation, stunted, stripped, and held captive within this nation."

Wright wrote at length about his resentment toward the Party, but these are retrospective comments. He remained in the Party, it should be noted, long after most of his literary friends had left it, even while he chafed under Party directives. That was the burden of his article, "I Tried to be a Communist." In this piece and in his contribution to *The God That Failed,* he drew a picture of a manipulating, opportunistic, sectarian-ridden Communist leadership whose ultimate purpose in bringing in intellectuals and writers was simply to turn them into instruments of propaganda—to convert them into 'weapons.'

He joined the Party, he tells us, when it still distrusted intellectuals and was sensitive to all manner of heresies and deviations, and almost from the beginning Wright began to challenge the Party line. He opposed the liquidation of the John Reed Clubs in 1935 and the Party decision to substitute in their place a more controllable literary ogranization, the League of American Writers. (The Clubs had become almost quasi-autonomous, and the Party leadership feared the Club magazines might open their columns too freely to left-wing deviationists). In 1937 Wright was certainly the Party's most illustrious proletarian author. All the same, it interfered with his literary work by imposing on him various extra-literary tasks. Still, if Wright (as he said in 1944) had become disenchanted with the Communists, if not their cause, as early as 1937, he continued to serve the Party faithfully even after 1939—a fact he omitted in his 1944 piece.

For example, in 1937 he wrote an essay entitled "Blue-Print for Negro writing" in which he called upon Black writers to stop distrusting each other and pled for "unity with all the progressive ideas of our day, the primary prerequisite for collective work." To achieve a progressive unity, to arrive at "a thorough integration with the American scene," the novelist needed a theory that would account for the "meaning, structure, and direction of modern society." Without this theory, the writer floundered. Once the Negro writer responded to the Marxian vision, he was granted "a sense of dignity" which "no other vision could give." It restored to him "his lost heritage, that is, his role as a creator of himself."

These were very fine words, so far as the Party theorists were concerned, and they praised the author of *Uncle Tom's Children* and *Native Son*—although Party critics were by no means unanimous in their opinions of the latter novel. When Wright declared that Marxism aided the writer to create the world in which he lived, that it restored his role "as a creator of himself," he was already treading on dangerous ground. Perhaps he thought the Party would be pleased with his formulation, but it is conceivable that even then he already suspected it might not accept his rather subjective notions about *his* world and the deliverance of his private self. Constance Webb's book on Wright lists excerpts from a talk entitled "Personalism" he delivered at a Midwest conference in 1936 or 1937. These also contain heretical ideas. There is no question but that the Party would have preferred Wright to supplement his themes of Negro exploitation with prophecies of white/Black proletarian solidarity along the lines followed by Paul Peters and George Sklar in *Stevedore.* In this play, an embattled group of Black New Orleans longshoremen are eventually joined by their white brothers in common resistance against the capitalist foe. Black proletarian and white proletarian, two massive figures featured in the *New Masses* cartoons, standing arm in arm—that's what the Party wanted.

The possibility of the Black man's legitimate hatred for capitalist exploitation existing side by side with hatred for whites of all political creeds never occurred to the Party leadership. Neither did it occur to them that they might be regarded as carriers of the racist virus. It is not unlikely that in the late Thirties Wright himself was living a kind of double intellectual life. One side of him—the Black Marxist, very likely a true believer in the Party's fight against its enemies at home and abroad—contributed useful articles and poems and stories to the Party press. The other and private side tried to explain and define the meaning of being Black in white America, tried to discover his own identity and in effect, to create himself.

After he left the Movement, the Party accused him of refashioning "the truths of his own life in a distorted and destructive image." They said the Richard Wright of 1934 was not the Richard Wright of 1944. In short, Wright lied when he wrote, "I Tried to be a Communist." Wright was not lying, and he really did try. His hidden and perhaps repressed opposition to the Party came out in *Native Son,* if not before.

The instant success of that novel, its world-wide coverage, the author's, bona fide Communist affiliation meant that Party critics almost of necessity had to praise it. So far as the Party was concerned, *Native Son,* with the exception of *The Grapes of Wrath,* was the most important fictional work of the decade. Yet even the Communists could not pretend *Native Son* was ideologically flawless as the gingerly criticism of the novel in the files of the *New Masses* attests.

Officially the Party "rejoiced" with the Negro people in hailing the "magnificent artistry" of *Native Son.* It had its shortcomings, to be sure. One critic regretted "the absence of characters who would balance the picture by showing Negroes whose rebellion against oppression is expressed in constructive mass action rather than in individual violence." Another thought the trial scene too long, and really unnecessary, for it only stated what had already been dramatically shown. To this legitimate objection he added, rather cautiously, that *Native Son* was not "an all-inclusive picture of Negro life" in America.

Other critics, however, took a more serious view of Wright's ideological lapses. The unfriendly critique came down to the following set of objections. The artist can't assume his task is completed after he has drawn his material from the physical world; subject matter of this sort is not axiomatically a true picture of reality. The author must build upon his esthetic perceptions if he is to achieve a broader fidelity. Aesthetics must be informed by politics. Is Bigger Thomas a representative of his people? Wright says he is—but the conception of Bigger is aesthetically false and politically confused:

> In *Native Son* Bigger is a frustrated, anti-social individual who commits anarchic acts of violence in his blind rebellion against capitalist society. It is politically slanderous to contend that Bigger Thomas is the symbol of the Negro people. Consequently it is an esthetic falsity to select a character who is atypical and to make him the protagonist of a novel that deals with the bitter persecution and exploitation of a minority people in bourgeois society.

Furthermore, Wright made Communists out to be insensitive fools like Jan and Mary. Even Boris Max never really understands Bigger, and is frightened by Bigger's vision of himself. Not a single white character, in fact, has any appreciation of what is going on in Bigger's mind.

Bigger dies defeated by society — not a fitting conclusion from the point of view of socialist realism, which usually posits a sunrise or a dawn at the end. Even sympathizers of the exploited Blacks would hesitate to accept Wright's justification of Bigger's behavior—" a repellant mystical confession of 'creation.' " And if readers in the Movement were not persuaded, how would the bourgeois subscribers to the Book of the Month Club respond?

To such ideologues, it did no good to point out that Wright did not address himself to that larger Communist reality or write to soothe the feelings of the Book of the Month Club readers. He had urged Black writers to write about what they knew and nothing else. His subject in *Native Son* was the Bigger Thomases of America. He was writing about a boy who had to hate in order to remain human, but of course such psychological or existential considerations cut no ice with the Party. Quite rightly, given its assumption, it saw something subversive and dangerous in *Native Son.*

By 1940 Wright had ended his literary apprenticeship. Literature had been his vehicle for discovering the world outside him and, more important, himself. Communism afforded only one of the roads to that territory from which the young Richard Wright had been excluded. But he had not succeeded in reconciling, either in his work or in his mind, the streams of influence that accounted for *Native Son*: Marxist universalism and Black nationalism. He paid lip service to the former, or, rather, he believed in it, acted on it, but he felt Black nationalism. It touched something deeper in his nature. Wright spoke from the heart when he said the Negro writer is "called upon to do no less than create values by which his race is to struggle, live and die..."

Richard Wright

MARGARET WALKER ALEXANDER

INTRODUCTION:

I first saw Richard Wright on Sunday afternoon, February 16, 1936, in Chicago at the Old Armory Building where he was presiding over the Writers' Section of the First National Negro Congress. I last saw him on the evening of June 9, 1939, in New York City where I had gone to attend the League of American Writers' Convention, see the New York World's Fair, and hopefully sell my novel, *Goose Island.* During those three years I think we were rather good friends. Looking back upon that relationship, it seems a rare and once-in-a-lifetime association which I am sure was not merely of mutual benefit but rather uncommon in its completely literary nature. And by "literary" I do not mean "arty" or pretentious or any form of dilettantism which he despised. I believe now that we shared a genuine interest in writing, in books, and literature. Moreover, we were mutually engaged in those three years in a number of associations and undertakings that, given the perspective of thirty-five years since their inception, seem uncanny in their significance.

We were writers together on the Federal Writers' Project of the WPA in Chicago; we were members of the South Side Writers' Group; we were interested in the little magazine, *New Challenge*; we had mutual friends and associates who were also writers; and during those three years we were struggling to publish for the first time in national magazines and books. We had varying and unequal degrees of success, but both of our talents found shape during those years. I know I owe much to his influence and interest in my writing and publishing poetry at that time: I am not so sure how much he owed to me. One thing I do know, however, is that during this three-year period Richard Wright wrote "Almos' A Man," *Lawd Today,* "The Ethics of Living Jim Crow," "Blueprint for Negro Writers," all the five stories in *Uncle Tom's Children,* and *Native Son.* Prior to our friendship, although he had published poetry in left-wing magazines, he had not published one significant piece of imaginative prose. I had the privilege of watching the birth of each of these works and seeing them through various stages of conception, organization, and realization. His first scissors and paste job was the first I had ever witnessed, and I rejoiced with him as each of these works found publication.

Langston Hughes originally introduced us (and when Wright died in Paris, Langston wrote me from London the news of their last visit). Wright in turn had introduced me to Arna Bontemps and Sterling Brown, who were on the WPA. In our South Side Writers' Group were Theodore Ward, the playwright, and Frank Marshall Davis, the poet, who was working for the Associated Negro Press. On the Project were such writers as Nelson Algren, whose sole work at that time was *Somebody in Boots,* Jacob Scher, James Phelan, Sam Ross, John T. Frederick, Katherine Dunham, Willard Motley, Frank Yerby, and Fenton Johnson.

Wright and I went to some of the same studio parties, read the same books, spent long evenings talking together, and often walked from the North Side where the Project was located, on Erie Street, downtown to the public library, or rode the El to the Southside where we lived. He gave me books for presents: an autographed manuscript of "Almos' A Man," a carbon copy of *Lawd Today*, which I had typed gratis; a copy of Flaubert's *Madame Bovary,* of e. e. cummings' *The Enormous Room,* and an autographed copy of *Uncle Tom's Children.* For two years after he went to New York we corresponded, and for the most part I kept his letters. My gifts were invariably of food and wine and cigarettes, and perhaps, what he valued most, an exchange of ideas, moral support and a steadfast encouragement, because I had no doubt from the beginning that he would win fame and fortune. When I met him his apprentice years were over and in that last year of his ten Chicago years it was easy to see where he was headed.

I

Going back in my memory to that Sunday afternoon in February, 1936, when I saw Wright for the first time, I remember that I went to the meeting because I heard it announced that Langston Hughes would be there. I met Langston first in New Orleans on his tour of the South in February, 1932, when he appeared in a Lecture Recital reading his poetry at the college, New Orleans University, where my parents taught. He encouraged me then to continue writing poetry and he also urged my parents to get me out of the deep South. Four years later to the very month, I wanted him to read what I had written in those four years. Six months earlier I had graduated from College at Northwestern and I still had no job. I was anxious to stay in Chicago where I hoped to meet other writers, learn something more about writing, and perhaps publish some of my poetry. I tried to press my manuscripts on Langston but when I admitted I had no copies he would not take them. Instead, he turned to Wright who was standing nearby, listening to the conversation and smiling at my desperation. Langston said, "If you people really get a group together, don't forget to include this girl." Wright promised that he would remember.

A month passed and I heard nothing. I presumed he had either forgotten or they didn't get a group together. Meanwhile on Friday, March 13, 1936, I received my notice in the mail to report to the WPA Writers' Project directed by Louis Wirth and located downtown in the Loop on Wells Street. Six weeks later I received a penny post card inviting me to the first meeting of the South Side Writers' Group. Twice I left the house and turned back the first time out of great self-consciousness because I felt I looked abominable. I had nothing to wear to make a nice appearance and I was going to the far Southside where I felt those people would make fun of me. But my great desire to meet writers and end my long isolation conquered this superficial fear. I made myself go. At the address given on the card, I discovered I was very late. I thought the meeting was over and I heard people laughing as I blurted out, "Is this the right place or am I too late?" I heard a man expounding on the sad state of Negro writing at that point in the thirties and he was punctuating his remarks with pungent epithets. I drew back in Sunday-school horror, totally shocked by his strong speech, but I steeled myself to hear him out. The man was Richard Wright. Subsequently, as each person present was asked to bring something to read next time, most people refused. When I was asked, I said, rather defiantly, that I would. I left the meeting alone.

Next time when we met at Lincoln Center on Oakwood Boulevard, I read a group of my poems. I was surprised to see they did not cut me down. Ted Ward and Dick Wright were kind in their praise. I remember Russell Marshall and Edward Bland were also there. Bland was killed in the battle of the Bulge. I was completely amazed to hear Wright read a piece of prose he was working on. Even after I went home I kept thinking, "My God, how that man can write!" After the meeting Wright said he was going my way. He asked me if I were on the Writers' Project, and I said, yes. Then he said, "I think I'm going to get on that Project." I looked at him in complete disbelief. I knew it took weeks and months to qualify for WPA plus additional red tape to get on one of the professional or art projects. What I did not know was that he had already been on WPA for some time. He was merely transferring from the Theatre Project to the Writers' Project.

The next week when I went to the Project Office for my semi-weekly assignment Wright was the first person I saw when I got off the elevator. He quickly came over and led me to his desk. He was a supervisor and I was a junior writer. My salary was $85 per month while his was $125. He hastened to explain that he was responsible for his mother, his aunt and his younger brother and he was, therefore, the head of a family though single, while I had only my sister as my responsibility. A year later I advanced to $94, but then he was getting ready to leave Chicago. Gradually a pattern established itself in our relationship on the Project. I went downtown twice weekly with my assignments on the Illinois Guide Book and afterward I spent most of the day in conversation with Wright. Sometimes I was there at the end of the day, but I never worked daily, as he did, in the office. I worked at home and went looking for news stories or covered art exhibits and made reports. And that is how I came to have a creative assignment after I had been on the Project about nine months. Wright, on the contrary, worked with the editorial group and sandwiched his writing in-between when there was a lull in office work. He had taught himself to type by the hunt and peck method and I was astounded to watch him type away with two or three fingers while his eyes concentrated on the keyboard.

The first writers' conference I attended was a Midwest Writers' Conference early in the Spring of 1936 shortly after I met Wright. He was speaking and asked me to attend. Afterwards in our South Side Writers' Group meeting I was recalling the incident and Frank Marshall Davis asked me if that wasn't a communist group. I was confused and said, "I don't know." Then I looked at Wright who only grinned gleefully and said, "Don't look at me!" The whole thing sank in gradually that he was a communist. I honestly didn't know what communism or Marxism meant. I had no courses in sociology, economics, nor political science while I was a student in college. I majored in English with emphasis on the European Renaissance and except for a few basic and general courses in mathematics, science, psychology, and religion, I concentrated on literature, history, and languages. My sister knew more about Hitler and Stalin than I did. I was even more puzzled when Jack Scher tried to give me some advice one afternoon leaving the Project. He said, "Margaret, I hope you will get to know all these people on the Project without getting to be a part of them and all they represent. You are young and you have talent. You can go far, so observe them but don't join them." Only years later did I begin to understand him. I thought he was seriously talking about the labor movement which was so exciting at that time. The C.I.O. was just being organized and I heard John L. Lewis speak several times. The A. F. of L. had never wanted Negroes in their trade unions. Wright seemed intensely interested in the labor struggle as well as all the problems of race and what he explained to me was a "class struggle."

One of the first books he handed me to read was John Reed's *Ten Days That Shook the World.* I was fascinated. That same summer Maxim Gorky died and I had never before heard the name. I read quickly his *Lower Depths* and *Mother* and then I read the so-called "Red" Archbishop of Canterbury's book, *The Soviet Power.* Having very little money to spend on books I bought them as I bought my clothes on lay-away and under the influence and partial tutelage of Wright I put five Modern Library Giant books in lay-away: Karl Marx's *Das Kapital,* Strachey's *The Coming Struggle for Power,* The Complete *Philosophy of Nietzsche,* Adam Smith's *The Wealth of Nations* and a novel by Romain Rolland. A whole year later and long after Wright was in New York, the books were mine. One afternoon Wright quoted from T. S. Eliot:

> Let us go then, you and I, when the evening is spread
> out against the sky
> like a patient etherized upon a table.

And he exclaimed, "What an image!" Something exploded in my head and I went home to find my copy of Untermeyer's anthology, *Modern American Poetry,* and re-read Eliot. I remember how dull he had seemed at Northwestern when the teacher was reading aloud, and even when I heard Eliot reading on a bad recording, "We are the hollow men . . ."

I began James Joyce with *Portrait of the Artist as a Young Man;* then read *Ulysses.* Wright used James Joyce as an example when he was writing *Lawd Today,* being struck by a book that kept all the action limited to one day, but he considered *Lawd Today,* which I retyped for him, as one of his worst works. I think it was actually his first completed novel. I remember that he regarded Melanchtha in Gertrude Stein's *Three Lives* as the first serious study of a Negro girl by a white American writer.

Stephen Crane's *Red Badge of Courage* I knew, but not *Maggie, Girl of the Streets* which was Wright's favorite. I think from the beginning we differed about Hemingway and Faulkner. Although I had read some of Hemingway, I had not read much of Faulkner and, despite Wright's ecstatic feeling about *Sanctuary,* I found it revolting, possibly because I was still strongly influenced by a moralistic and puritanical background.

I never worshipped at the altars of either Hemingway or Faulkner but Wright deeply admired both. I read James Farrell's *Studs Lonigan* at Wright's request, but I could not work up a passion for Clifford Odets' *Waiting For Lefty* which the WPA Theatre Project had produced while Wright was working for the Theatre Project in Chicago as well as Caldwell's *Kneel to the Rising Sun.* Caldwell's *Tobacco Road* was a nationally famous play and a Pulitzer Prize winner as was Paul Green's *In Abraham's Bosom* which I particularly liked. John Dos Passos' *The Big Money* and Sandburg's *The People, Yes,* were current favorites that we both loved. Reading Proust was an experience I associate completely with Wright. Wright's favorite D. H. Lawrence was *Sons and Lovers* rather than *Lady Chatterley's Lover:* I confess now that my understanding of *Sons and Lovers* was much better when I was much older, best of all after I became the mother of sons. But I am sure all this must have led to some discussions we had then of Freud, Jung, and Adler, especially of Freud. Also it is very important to remember when we read the later Richard Wright in a book like *The Outsider,* written after his association with Sartre, that way back there in the thirties he was intensely interested in Nietzsche, Schopenhauer, and above all, the novelist Dostoevski. Wright and I differed keenly on our taste and interest in the Russian writers. He believed that Dostoevski was the greatest novelist who ever lived and the *Brothers Karamazov* was his greatest novel. I never felt quite that extravagantly about him, even though I plunged into the book at that period for the first time. Turgenev and Conrad were two others on whom we differed. I had read some of both but now I found a renewed interest, but I have never felt as sympathetic toward Conrad as Wright did. I liked the element of adventure in his sea-tales such as *Typhoon* but I have never liked the short fiction; I realize now that I have deeply resented what I feel is ersatz in Conrad's treatment of Africa and the Negro. The two works Wright and I discussed most were *Lord Jim* and *The Nigger of the Narcissus.*

If there were two literary books that were Wright's Bible they were Henry James' *Collected Prefaces* on *The Art of the Novel* and Joseph Warren Beach's *Twentieth Century Novel.* It must have been James who first interested him in the long short story or the short novel which he correctly called by the Italian name, the novella. When we consider, however, that Wright was also familiar with the short fiction of Dostoevski, Flaubert, Melville, D. H. Lawrence, Joyce, and Mann as well as James, one cannot be too certain who first led him in this direction. I know, however, that he had been interested in the short story form for a very long time. I vaguely remember and realize now that he loved Edgar Allan Poe, A. Conan Doyle and Jack London, and that he talked of having read pulps, detective stories, and murder mysteries, long before his serious reading began with Mencken while he lived in Memphis. He was tremendously impressed with Mencken and I never read his essay on "Puritanism in American Literature" without thinking of Wright.

Suspended in time somewhere between the Writers' Project and the South Side Writers' Group, possibly in the parlor of the house where I lived, three forms of writing took place in our consciousness, conversation and actions. We sat together and worked on the forms of my poetry, the free verse things, and came up with my long line or strophic form, punctuated by a short line. I remember particularly the poem, "People of Unrest," which Wright and I revised together, emphasizing the verbs:

> Stare from your pillow into the sun
> See the disk of light in shadows.
> Watch day growing tall
> Cry with a loud voice after the sun.
> Take his yellow arms and wrap them round your life.

Be glad to be washed in the sun.
Be glad to see.
People of Unrest and sorrow
Stare from your pillow into the sun.

Likewise we sat together and worked on revisions of "Almos' A Man" and *Lawd Today.* We discussed the difficulties of Negro dialect, and Wright decided he would leave off all apostrophes and the usual markings for sight dialect. We discussed folk materials and the coincidence of our interest in Negro spirituals and the work songs and what Wright called the dozens (Cf. the opening lines of "Big Boy Leaves Home"). I remember both of us were working on a piece using the words of the spiritual "Down By The Riverside." "Silt" was a forerunner of the long short story "Down By The Riverside" which Wright wrote that same year. I felt hopeless about my novel manuscript which became *Jubilee* and of which I had 300 pages in first draft written at that time. We both decided I should put it away until another time.

I was pleasantly surprised to learn early in January of 1937 that I would be granted a creative writing assignment and my novel chapters could now be turned in as my work assignments. The day I was told, Wright was absent from work and I learned he was at home ill with a bad cold. When I went home that afternoon my sister and I decided to buy some oranges and take them to him. Then I could tell him my wonderful good news. We found him in the house on Indiana Avenue in bed in a room that I could not understand because it had one door and no windows. Imagine my shock when I later realized it was a closet. He was very happy to hear about my good luck and both of us were embarrassed about the oranges.

One cold windy day in Chicago, walking downtown from Erie Street, we crossed Wacker Drive, turning our backs to the wind, and went into the Public Library at Washington and Michigan Avenue. I was returning a pile of books and Richard said he felt tempted to teach me how to steal but he would resist such corruption. I assured him that I felt no compulsion to steal books.

II

Wright left Chicago for New York on May 28, 1937. It was Friday afternoon and payday on the Project. We generally went to the same check-cashing place nearby and when we were standing in line for checks Wright was behind me, so he asked me to wait for him. About that time one of the silly young gushing girls on the Project came up to me (as Nelson Algren used to say, "Dames who don't know the day of the week") and she said, "Margaret, tell Dick he's got to kiss all us girls goodbye." I laughed at her and told her, "Tell him yourself, I wouldn't dare!" When I got my check, I looked around and sure enough all the young white chicks were mobbing him with loving farewells—so I left. Outside on the street I had walked a block when I heard him yelling and hailing me. I turned and waited. "I thought I told you to wait for me?" he grinned impishly. I said, "Well, you were very busy kissing all the girls goodbye. I'm in a hurry. The currency exchange will close." We cashed the checks and got on the El. Fortunately the car was not crowded and we got seats on one of the long benches. He said, "When I go tonight, I will have forty dollars in my pocket."

"Oh, you are leaving tonight?"

"Yes, I've got a ride and lucky for me, it's a good thing 'cause I surely can't afford the railroad fare."

"Well, you'll make it."

"I hope I can get on the Writers' Project there. I've got to find work right away, and I hope I'm not making a mistake, going this way."

"How can you say such a thing? Aren't you on your way to fame and fortune? You can't be making a mistake."

"I knew you would say that. I guess you won't think again about coming to New York too, and soon."

"No, I've got to help my sister. I can't leave now."

"I think together we could make it big." He was not being sentimental and I didn't misunderstand him. I said, "I know you will make it big, but I can't leave now. Later, perhaps I will."

"You know, Margaret, I got a notice to come for permanent work at the Post Office, and I sat in my room and tore it up. Bad as I need money it was the hardest decision I ever made in my life."

"Well, would you like to be a postman all your life?" He looked at me and laughed. He didn't need to answer, for he had said more than once, "I want my life to count for something. I don't want to waste it or throw it away. It's got to be worthwhile."

His stop came first and suddenly he grabbed both my hands and said goodbye. That was Friday afternoon, and Tuesday I received his first letter. It was very brief, saying he had arrived Saturday and at first felt strange in the big city but in a little while he was riding the subways like an old New Yorker. He thought he had a lead on a job—in any case he would try Monday—and meanwhile, I must write him all the news from Chicago and tell him everything that was going on on the project; and like every letter that followed it was signed, *As ever, Dick.* I was surprised to get that letter. I never really expected that he would write, but I answered. My letters were generally longer, and I felt sometimes silly and full of gossip, but he continued to write often, if sometimes quite briefly.

In the Fall of 1937, he wrote that he was entering the WPA short story contest sponsored by *Story* Magazine and Harper's publishing house. I was supposed to enter *Goose Island* myself but I didn't get it ready in time. Wright had written all four of his novellas before going to New York. When he left he was working on "Bright and Morning Star," which was first published in *New Masses,* but it was not ready when he submitted the manuscript for the contest. "Big Boy Leaves Home" was the only story that had already been published; it appeared first in *American Caravan* while he was still on the Project in Chicago. He had also published "The Ethics of Living Jim Crow" in *American Stuff.* Earlier he had published poetry in *International Literature* and it was in that Russian magazine that both of us first read Sholokhov's *And Quiet Flows The Don.*

I don't think Wright ever wanted to write socialist realism, and he chafed under the dictates of the Communist Party to do so. If he had any aspirations beyond that, as he indicated after *Native Son,* it was toward his own unique form of symbolism. I don't think it came as a surprise when Wright won the short story contest though he had written once that it seemed a long time since he had submitted the manuscript and he hadn't heard anything. His friends in Chicago and New York were pleased and excited, but not surprised. They took it as a matter of course that his work was the best from all those sent in from WPA Projects around the country.

In November I published for the first time in *Poetry* magazine. Wright wrote at once that he had seen the poem, "*For My People,*" written in the summer after he left, and he liked it very much. Meanwhile, we were getting things together for *New Challenge* magazine. He wrote that I should send my manuscript of poems somewhere besides Yale. There were lots of other places, he said, and I should give up trying them, for after all they weren't likely to publish me or any other black person.

In the Spring of 1938, *Uncle Tom's Children* was published and Wright won the $500 prize. The book got interesting reviews, but all of them did not make us happy. He had moved to Lefferts Place and was staying with Jane and Herbert Newton. Then, on the wings of success came the news that he was getting married. I hastened to congratulate him, and he denied the whole thing. I learned later that the young, black, and very bourgeois girl he was dating thought Wright was even more successful in a financial way than he was. He had arranged to rent extra space from the Newtons and move his bride in with them but her family wanted her to have the best and if he couldn't provide that—no soap. Well, it was no soap. Regardless of financial status, in one year after his arrival in New York he had achieved national prominence. He remarked in a letter at the end of that year that he had set a goal for five years and one of those years was over. He wanted to write another book right away, a novel, before the first one could be forgotten. Then he wanted to go to Mexico and he wanted to go to Paris.

During the first week in June, 1938, I received in rapid

succession two airmail special delivery letters. I answered one at once but before he could receive my answer he wrote again in great excitement. He said, "I have just learned of a case in Chicago that has broken there and is exactly like the story I am starting to write. See if you can get the newspaper clippings and send them to me." The case was that of a young black boy named Nixon who had been accused of rape, and when the police captured him they forced a confession of five major crimes, of which rape was only one.

I went at once to the offices of the five daily Chicago newspapers to get all the back issues; and I began what lasted a year, sending Wright every clipping published in the newspapers on the Nixon case. Frankly, there were times when the clippings were so lurid I recoiled from the headlines, and the details in the stories were worse. They called Nixon a big black baboon. When I went into news offices or bought papers on the stands, I listened to jeers and ugly insults about all black people.

Meanwhile, Wright wrote that if I had anything I wanted published to send it to him and he would push my work, as he was now in a better position to help me get published. He had already read many of my assignments on *Goose Island* before leaving Chicago; and he suggested that I might send him more.

Not until Wright visited in November did I learn how he had made use of the newspaper clippings. Actually, the case rocked on for about a year. In the fall of 1938, Wright wrote that he would have to make a trip home to Chicago before he could finish the book. One Sunday in November, when I entered the house, my landlady said, "There is a surprise for you in the living room." I said, "A surprise for me? What kind of surprise?" I had come out of a bright day outside and the living room looked dim and shadowy. I squinted my eyes to see and Wright laughed, "Poor little Margaret, she doesn't even know me."

He had only stopped in his mother's house long enough to put down his bag. He washed his hands and ate with us—a quick meal of chicken and biscuits, soup and salad. Then he went out into the streets, visited his friends, the Gourfains, and found a vacant lot to use for the address of the Dalton house in *Native Son.* I thought we were walking aimlessly when we found ourselves at a little tea-room and we went inside. It was late Sunday afternoon—twilight or dusk and the little bell on the door tinkled to let the keeper know we were entering. There were only two people inside—a man wiping cups and the proprietor; but one knew Wright and we sat down at a table. Soon other men entered; the room began to fill with white men. Gradually I felt acutely that I was the only woman in the room.

Wright explained a little about the new book and told about the clippings. He said he had enough to spread all over his nine by twelve bedroom floor and he was using them in the same way Dreiser had done in *American Tragedy.* He would spread them all out and read them over and over again and then take off from there in his own imagination. The major portion of *Native Son* is built on information and action of those clippings. One of the men asked him where he got the clippings and he looked at me and said, "She sent them to me." A mutual friend, Abe Aaron said, "You ought to dedicate the book to her" and I quickly said, "I'd kill him if he did. He's going to dedicate it to his mother." Wright said, "How did you know that?" But of course he did. Later he wrote, and I quote:

> I felt guilty as all hell for not writing to you, inasmuch as you had done more than anyone I know to help me with my book. Nearly all the newspaper releases in the book were sent to me by you. Each and every time I sat down to write I wondered what I could say to let you know how deeply grateful I felt.

All in all, Wright was a man of great personal magnetism and charm. Women and men adored him. He could charm the socks off of anyone and everyone he bothered to notice.

He asked me that Sunday if I had a little time to spend helping him find things for the book and I readily assented. On Monday we did several things. First, we went to visit Attorney Ulysses S. Keyes who had expressed an interest in meeting Wright and had once asked me to let him know whenever Wright came to town. He was the first black lawyer hired for Nixon's defense. He had also written a fan letter to Wright and when we went to his office he was quite glad to see the author of *Uncle Tom's Children.* I asked him about the Nixon case and if he wasn't the defense lawyer on the case. He said, "I was until this morning. The family has hired an NAACP lawyer, and after I had written the brief and everything." I then asked him if he would give it to Wright. All this time Wright said nothing and when I asked for the brief Wright looked at me as if I were crazy and I guess I was, but when we were outside I said, "Well, wasn't that what you needed?" He said, "Yes, but I didn't have the nerve to ask that man for his brief." But of course he found good use for it.

Next we went visiting Cook County Jail where Nixon was incarcerated. I nearly fainted when I saw the electric chair for the first time. Outside, we snapped pictures, but I still felt weak. On the elevated train we looked out over Southside rooftops and Wright explained that he had his character running across those rooftops. I asked, why? And Wright said, "He's running from the police." I said, "Oh, that must be dramatic to the point of melodrama." He said, "Yes, I think it will shock people, and I love to shock people!" He grinned gleefully and rubbed his hands together in anticipation, and I couldn't stop laughing.

The next day we went to the Library and checked out on my library card two books we found on the Loeb-Leopold case and on Clarence Darrow, their lawyer. The lawyer's defense of Bigger in *Native Son* was modeled after Darrow's defense. Wright was so long sending those books back that I wrote him a hot letter reminding him that I had not borrowed those books permanently! He finished the book early in the Spring of 1939 and he wrote that he had never worked so hard before in all his life.

> Listen, from the time I left Chicago and got back to New York, I worked from 7, 8, 9, in the morning until 12, 1, 2 and 3 at night. I did that for day in and day out. Sometimes I worked so hard that my mind ceased to register and

> I had to take long walks. I never intend to work that long and hard again. If this book is published, then I'll delay getting my next one out, for two reasons: I'm making a new departure and I don't want to kill myself. But I had to get that book out and I wanted it out before the first was forgotten. Rest assured, that if this book is published, you'll *hear* about it. The liberals, the CP, the NAACP—all of them will have their reservations. Really, I don't believe that they are going to publish it. Really, I don't even though they've signed the contract. . .

And again he wrote:

> Yes, I'm beginning another book, but sort of half-heartedly. I'm trying to wait and see what in hell they are going to do with the last one. The title is "Native Son." I don't like the title. They have had it for a week now and I have not heard what they are planning; that is, I don't know if they are going to publish it late Spring or early Fall. The new book will be a sharp departure in my work. I feel that I've gone as far as I care to go with Negro characters of the inarticulate type. Within the next ten or fifteen days I'll hear from Guggenheim. Also I'll know if I can stay at Yaddo, an artist colony, free for a few weeks of rest.

And according to my journal entries I note that he wrote a few days later that he had gotten the Guggenheim! He asked me again about coming to New York and this time, with *Goose Island* finished, I said I was considering it. I have forgotten to say that when he was in Chicago in November, I had discovered the plot of *Native Son* while I was cooking that Sunday afternoon, and I turned to him, stricken, and said, "Oh, we are doing the same thing. The only difference is your main character is a man and mine is a woman." He said, "No matter, there's room enough for both" and he buttered another hot biscuit. But I was quite apprehensive and told him so. My fiction was not nearly as well formed and advanced as his, and I felt from that moment that *Goose Island* was doomed. The goose was cooked!

Then, quite without notice, about the middle of May, he turned up in Chicago again for a few days. His younger brother, Alan, was ill with bleeding ulcers and Wright had come to see about him. He asked me then about my plans for the trip, and said he would be speaking on Friday evening at the League Convention and hopefully I would be there then. We even discussed riding on the train together, but I said I was not quite ready. I was having real money problems and I did not want to tell him I might not be able to make it. One of the things I promised to do was read the manuscript of *Native Son* as I had read everything else he had written in manuscript before that, but I never quite got the time. I know I would have violently protested against the end of *Native Son,* although my protests would probably not have helped. I'm sure that was a revised ending. I don't think it was in character for an unconscious character such as Bigger Thomas to analyze his circumstance or situation in such conscious terms. It was obviously a Marxist ending made for socialist realism and not for the naturalistic piece of fiction that *Native Son* is. I can't believe that Wright didn't also know that it was wrong, and too contrived an ending.

Wright wrote a piece in *Saturday Review of Literature* called "How Bigger Was Born," and perhaps that character did evolve in his mind for a long time from his childhood and youth in the violent South; but I have told you how *Native Son* evolved from the Nixon Case and sociological research done long before Wright began writing his story.

I sometimes ask myself if I had not made the trip to New York that June of 1939, would we have remained friends. I think not. Everything seemed destined toward an end of those three years, for whatever the relationship was worth. At first I was hurt deeply, and pained for many years. The memory of that trip is still too painful to discuss, but as I have grown older and look back in maturity over those three years I know what happened was best for me.

III

Wright's philosophy was that fundamentally all men are potentially evil. Every man is capable of murder or violence and has a natural propensity for evil. Evil in nature and man are the same; nature is ambivalent and man may be naturally perverse and as quixotic as nature. Human nature and human society are determinants and, being what he is, man is merely a pawn caught between the worlds of necessity and freedom. He has no freedom of choice; he is born to suffering, despair, and death. He is alone against the odds of Nature, Chance, Fate and the vicissitudes of life. All that he has to use in his defense and direction of his existence are (1) his reason and (2) his will. By strength of reason and will he can operate for the little time he has to live.

His philosophy developed as a result of his experiences: he turned against orthodox religion at an early age because of the religious fanaticism in his family and early home-life. He grew up in a South where lynching and Jim Crow and every egregious form of racism were rampant; and the fate of a Black Boy was not only tenuous or nebulous, but often one of doom. To be poor and black in an hostile white world was his first knowledge of the human condition and he found that living in a rural area or in an urban area made no difference. His piece on "The Ethics of Living Jim Crow" drives this home long before the autobiography *Black Boy.* The five novellas that eventually form the second edition of *Uncle Tom's Children* were all of one piece: the tragic fate of a black man in the hostile white world of a violent South land. The title *Uncle Tom's Children* is a misnomer and misleading. It is an abominable title chosen as usual by the publishers. That book should never have been associated with Uncle Tom. It bears no resemblance to *Uncle Tom's Cabin,* the book or the minstrel play. Any one of the stories would have made a better title for the book. But to get back to the point, *Native Son's* bitterness is even more intense because Bigger is in a bigger bear trap than Bobo and Big Boy. He is in *big* Chicago, poor, black, ignorant, and scared! He has no hope of being able to cope with the big white rich man's world in the big city. He blunders into crime. He is driven by such desperate fear he cannot imagine himself as a human being of dignity and worth. He begs the question. He is unconscious, inarticulate, and confused.

Wright developed a cautious and suspicious nature. He said it was part of his protective coloring but that suspicion of everybody grew as he grew older and it was not unlike that of many philosophers who hold secular or materialist positions. They have no faith in anybody, God, Man, or the devil. He was not nihilistic but he partook of some of its negativism. He was completely a secularist and secular existentialism was his final belief. It is best expressed in what I regard as his most autobiographical piece, *The Outsider.* Cross Damon has a lot of Richard Wright in him that Bigger Thomas was not big enough to understand.

All the forces influencing Wright were forces of the white world: he seems to have been shaped very little by black people. As a matter of fact black people were never his ideals. He championed the cause of the black man but he never idealized or glorified him. His black men as characters were always seen as the victims of society, demeaned and destroyed and corrupted to animal status. He was the opposite of what the liberal white man is called: a nigger lover. He probably never reached the point of hating his black brothers, but he felt himself hated by many of them. Every positive force he recognized in his life stemmed from white forces. Intellectually his teachers and master-models were all white. He was befriended by whites; he was admired and loved more by whites than blacks. Hatred of the collective white man as a force against the collective black man was nevertheless coupled with genuine admiration and regard for many truly personal benefactors who were white. I sometimes wonder if it is malicious to think he would have been happier if he had been born white than he was as a black man. He seemed to feel and believe that all his troubles stemmed from being black. Unlike Langston Hughes, who loved all mankind and especially his black brothers, Wright often said that there was no kind of cruelty worse than black people could inflict on their own people. His favorite authors were all white. I cannot think of a single black author during the thirties whom he admired to the point that he considered him the equal of any white writer. He had no great respect for the literary achievements of black people, not even Langston Hughes or W. E. B. DuBois. Many black writers admired him, but when he picked his friends among writers they were all white. He certainly had no high regard for black nationalism despite his interests in Africa and Asia. He was not a nationalist but an internationalist.

Wright's greatest influence, however, has been on black writers. A new school of naturalistic novelists and symbolists, all black, came out of the thirties and the forties because of Wright. Those most often mentioned and their works are Ann Petry, Willard Motley, Chester Himes, James Baldwin, and Ralph Ellison. I think it is safe to say that at least in fiction of the Twentieth Century in Black America we can mark or date everything before and after Richard Wright. Like the Russians who say they have all come out of Gogol's "Overcoat," most of our writers have come out of Wright's cloak.

Re-reading the early fiction of Wright one is struck by the passion and the power that always come through. These were also in his early poetry, the remarkable "Between the World and Me" and "I Have Seen Black Hands," two poems he wrote before he turned to Haiku, a form I cannot conceive as being Wright's despite his experimenting in countless poems with it. In his short factual prose pieces, articles, book reviews, news articles, and pot-boiling bits of journalism and propaganda one is always aware of the curious almost mercurial vitality that his writing possessed. Wright really began his imaginative writing career as a poet, although he never in life published a book of poetry. He understood quite well the craft and technique of poetry, particularly free verse. He read and loved poetry purely for enjoyment and relaxation. Once, going on a train trip, he took along Whitman's *Leaves of Grass* to read for pure pleasure. He was quite familiar with the poets of the thirties such as Muriel Rukeyser and Robinson Jeffers. Once he invited me to go with him to hear Kenneth Fearing. He liked T. S. Eliot, Yeats, Sandburg, Masters, and even Ezra Pound. He wrote back once from New York how he was reading the *Road to Xanadu,* an adventure in the imagination, and also for the first time, *Alice in Wonderland.*

Wright would have been the last person to argue his gift of inner perception, for he also wrote this to me:

> You know, Margaret, writing does not mean that one has a masterful grip on all of life. After all, writing comes primarily from the imagination; it proceeds from that plane where the world and brute fact and feeling meet and blend. In short, a writer may exhibit a greater knowledge of the world than he has actually seen. That may sound like a paradox. . . . This is not irony. Hence, the alertness which should be mine, the sharpness of attention which people say it takes to write, that depth which people find in one's books, well, it simply is not there. . . . I am not subtle, even though there might be imaginative subtleties in my work. Imagination is truer than life; that is the fact which every writer discovers and the fact which people usually concede to the conscious mind of the writer. . . . Frankly, Margaret, what you see and feel in my work is something which everybody has and which, for some reason I don't really understand, gets itself on paper somehow. So don't expect me in my daily relations with folks to have the same strength of vision and awareness you see or think you see in my work. I'm answering this from an odd angle but I feel it is the angle which settles things. I take the world at its face value far more often than you will ever know. Maybe I'll see you again this summer and we'll talk more at length; and I won't be so hurried and worried as I was last time. . . .

The white scholar today who finds Wright a fit subject for study says he cannot understand the apathy of black scholars toward Richard Wright. What he fails to say is that the black writer has been profoundly influenced by Wright, impressed with his success and made confident and bold because of his intellectual honesty. Many black scholars have in truth written interesting articles if not books about Wright, but the black scholar does not in truth subscribe to the belief that we should bow down before this black god and worship his black genius, for some of us have known the man and we know that all men are made of clay.

New York

Personal Impressions

HENRIETTA WEIGEL:

It was in the early or mid-thirties, I think, when I first met Richard Wright, though I had really met him before—through his unpublished stories that later were printed under the title of *Uncle Tom's Children* and won the Harper's prize.

I had been working part-time for a literary agent (now dead), to whom Wright had sent these stories from Chicago, where he had been living after leaving the South. The agent was a very rich man, more interested in meeting writers than in marketing their stories. My chores included the reading of mss. that were usually buried in the drawers of exquisite Japanese cabinets. Wright's stories were fresh, startling, and swelled my anger against the agent, who had done nothing about trying to market them.

One day old friends, living in Chicago, drove to New York City in their dilapidated car. Richard Wright had come along with them. My husband and I were living on Bleecker Street. It was the time of the Depression; we were young, spirited, and dedicated to making a better world. Wright was sullen, suspicious (though not with Herbert and Isabelle, the white married couple whose car he had shared). They were all tired and dusty, as well as hungry, after the long trip. John, my husband, and I suggested they shower and freshen themselves while we made dinner. We gave each one a clean bath towel. Wright said, "Me too?"—evidently wondering whether he was included in our hospitality. We made it clear he was, though we were embarrassed by his question. We had friends among all races and nations; the world seemed simpler then, or perhaps we were. We felt closer to those who shared our enthusiasm for change than to our own conventional families.

It was only at the end of the evening, after we had had drinks and food and wine and talk, and when our guests were about to leave that it occurred to me to ask Dick Wright whether he wrote!

He did: the stories I had read were his. I suggested he retrieve them from the agent, and take them to an acquaintance who was at that time working for the Reynolds literary agency. It was the latter agents who brought his stories to the (then) Harper's publishing company. It seems needless to add that I had little to do really with the stories' success that followed. Wright got to know many people (and got a job with WPA, a haven for artists during the Depression).

Dick had only one suit then, and in celebration of the Harper's prize bought himself a new one, with 2 pairs of trousers (at Barney's). He came to visit and showed us the newspaper-wrapped treasure. When we questioned him about the newspaper-wrapping, he said he had specially requested it since in the South clothes bought by blacks were always wrapped that way. He refused to open the package, but allowed us to scratch an opening through which we could see an infinitesimal part of the suit.

His attitude towards us changed: he accepted our friendship, and many of our friends became his, too. Wright was attractive; he alternated between sullenness, when he felt rejected by whites (stupid though they might be), and volatile warmth when sensing kinship in spirit. Then he would share his vivid imagination, talking freely of work either in progress or that he wanted to do in the future.

I recall his enthusiasm about a book he had begun (never finished, I believe). The heroine, black, wanted to be white, and had begun taking treatments with a white doctor-scientist who, through a daring formula, could transform her color.

At parties Dick never joined the groups of people dancing. He seemed like a deacon at those times, silently condemning his people for being what he considered "court jesters" in the white world.

He was not averse to punishing white friends, including myself, by becoming remote and rude when he had suffered rebuffs from whites. At one gathering near Sutton Place where we went together, a white young woman scanned the comics in the newspaper, ignoring the "intellectual" conversation going on. Dick Wright was the only black present, and though genuinely admired and liked by the men who hosted the party, he lectured the young woman on her lack of social concern.

We had travelled downtown by bus. After I was seated, he retreated to the back of the bus, ignoring me. When we got out, he walked quite a distance behind me. He told me later that he had not wanted to disgrace me in the bus by letting me be seen with a black man. He had, furthermore, walked behind (not with) me in the street to save me from embarrassment. I remembered then that Negroes in the South either rode in the back of busses or in segregated ones. I had visited the South once, and fled in shame at being a member of the white race.

At one time, Dick Wright, two black young women (one of whom was an anthropologist to whom he was attracted, but who did not return his affection), Claude McKay, and myself, started a magazine, *New Challenge.* We could only get out two issues because the funds we had collected were used up, and furthermore McKay and Wright disagreed violently on politics (Wright was then still an ardent Communist).

He was attracted to white women, and felt they were stronger than white men. He married two: the first a dancer; then Ellen.

I first met Jimmy Baldwin, before he was published, at a gathering at Kenneth Fearing's, and we became friends. I read *Go Tell It To The Mountain* in ms. I introduced him to Wright but they were cool to each other. I was disappointed, childishly believing that Wright, having experienced the difficulties of being a black writer in the USA, would at once take Baldwin "under his wing."

During the time Wright was living in Brooklyn Heights, renting a room from the Newtons, I visited him. Ellen, to whom he was not yet married, was there also. I became so fascinated with Mrs. Newton that I spent all of that visit with her. She was a white woman who had married a black man; she was a member of a socially prominent Chicago family that had attempted to have her declared insane for marrying a black man, but the psychiatrists proved them wrong. She seemed hungry for sympathetic companionship. She showed me the poems she wrote; she said her forefathers had fought in the Civil War for freedom, and she was carrying on their tradition by marrying a black man.

When I told this to Dick, he responded angrily, saying that Mrs. Newton thought so little of herself that only a black man could be her husband—then, at least, she could feel superior to someone. However, despite this demolishment of Mrs. Newton, he helped her with money and kindness when she was ill (and parted from Mr. Newton).

When Dick went abroad to live with Ellen and their children, we lost touch. Somehow, I felt he needed *not* to exile himself. He was an American; his prophetic anger, birthed by this country, was interwoven with his great talent. I am not a scholar, but it seems to me that the existentialist philosophy had not yet been fully digested by him. It was not indigenous to him or his art. No matter, though, for he was a fine artist, achieving universality through his discovery in writing of all people's suffering, illuminating a world still to be explored.

BENJAMIN APPEL:

I think it was Ralph Ellison who told me that Dick Wright was living around the corner from me—on Middagh Street in Brooklyn Heights. A very young Ellison back then in 1942—fame still around the corner for him—one of the many beginning writers, white and Negro (black was still a color and not a race) who revolved around the author of *Native Son*.

I had met Wright at parties, at the Congresses of the League of American Writers, but that was all. A handshake, a drink, a little conversation. Ellison, as Wright's friend, was the middleman who brought us together.

Middagh was a white man's street in white Brooklyn Heights, and Ellison was worried about what people, some of them anyway, would think of the new family who had moved into the first floor apartment of a house owned by Carson McCullers.

There might be ugly words, maybe incidents.

Especially since Wright's wife was a white woman whose baby as I would be told later by an Angry White Woman had been tarred black.

I had just moved to Brooklyn Heights myself but I promised Ellison to do what I could. For example: people on Brooklyn Heights read books and Wright was a fine writer, etc.

Up with Literature! And I might add up with Democracy!

America was at war with Japan and Nazi Germany. Press and radio, a thousand voices proclaimed democracy, brotherhood, and an end to fascism and the fascist doctrines of "inferior" and "subhuman" races.

Dick Wright, as I got to know him better, had his doubts about the democracy-shouters. If he was drafted, he said, he would refuse to serve. He would refuse to serve unless Britain immediately gave India her independence. No soldiering for him in a white man's war unless—ah, that memorable *unless*—the US Army granted him an officer's commission.

His eyes usually so sad and introspective would change into those of an extrovert, militant and military. As if he heard bugles: Lieutenant Richard Wright. . . .

1942 was a year of disaster and defeat for the anti-Fascist coalition. There was a feeling, a dread of worse to come, all of us on board a scuttled ship, and who knew if any of us would be saved.

Wright, as a Negro *and* a poet, had his very own special anxieties. He was working on a new novel whose characters quite literally had gone underground to live in sewers. I'd drop in on him and as he spoke about his novel, the brownstone street outside, genteel Brooklyn Heights with its marble fireplaces of an earlier New York, would float off like smoke.

Years later after reading Kafka's *The Trial* I realized that Dick Wright had staged his own trial. And as his own judge turned in a verdict of Guilty. What did it matter that he wasn't guilty? To be a Negro was guilt enough in USA 1942.

His child had been born in the Brooklyn Jewish Hospital, and Wright's wife, Jewish herself, had overheard the nurses talking about *somebody* who'd had a black baby. They didn't know *she* was the *one.* And when they found out, Mrs. Wright counted the days like a prisoner.

The white uniforms. For Dick Wright there was no escaping them, they came after him in his dreams, and after his child, guilty too because of color. Repetitious dreams of white men, white monsters. *Whiteness* shook him awake and he would hurry into his child's room. No, *they* hadn't taken her away, not this time. Safe! Often, as he told me, he would sleep in the same room next to his baby.

Whiteness was the spook in Dick Wright's woodpile—to paraphrase the old and hatefilled saying.

Whiteness had to be met, overcome, defeated. As it had been in *Native Son.* In that famous novel, Bigger (a revealing name!) murders the spook who here has assumed the form of a beautiful girl, whiter than white almost, not because of her fair skin and blonde hair but because of her social status. If Bigger is at the bottom, another and almost nameless Negro in slumland, his victim, a debutante, an American princess, is living in the snowwhite castles of w.a.s.p.-land. In the original draft, Wright said, Bigger'd raped the girl before killing her. I can't recall whether it was editor or publisher who convinced Dick to unrape (my phrase) Bigger's victim.

Fame and money—he had them both. He'd come a long way from the Mississippi boy who in Chicago discovered the Revolution, and the Communist Party. More than a Party for him, a house where he, a Negro, first sat at table with white folks instead of fetching in the dishes. Like so many Communists who had lost the faith he saw devils where there had only been angels. Once his wife remarked that Dick wouldn't even read the *Worker,* that his favorite paper was the *News.* She bought them all at the corner news-stand.

He distrusted the press (certain only of violence and sensation as it was reported in the tabloid), distrusted the war leaders, Roosevelt, Churchill, Stalin, distrusted all political parties and all political promises.

Only an individual could be depended upon, only an individual could be straight—even a white cop in Harlem. This isn't just an extravagant figure of speech. In the spring of 1942 a young white cop—now long retired from the force—had while on duty shot and killed a Negro psychotic.

I knew this cop or rather had known him when I lived in Hell's Kitchen, the West Side of Manhattan, another kid on my block. And there he was headline news. A hero in the *Daily News;* a "Gestapo cop" in the *Amsterdam News* and other Negro publications. He came to see me to plead his case; he had killed in self-defense and most certainly wasn't a "Gestapo cop." A Jewish cop, in fact, liberal in his politics. He had read some of my novels (and a few years later I would fictionize him in a novel about a race riot, *The Dark Stain,* a fan, in short. Since I had become an author, he concluded, mistakenly, that I must know Big & Influential People. The Mayor of New York perhaps. Adam Clayton Powell, Jr. and other famous Negro leaders. . . . He felt that if he could talk to them, explain what really happened, then his name would be cleared.

I didn't know the Mayor, etc. But I arranged a meeting with Dick Wright. Dick was convinced, he spoke to influential Negro leaders, did what he could as an individual to help another individual.

With summer I moved from Brooklyn Heights, and the war would carry me as so many others, to other scenes. I never saw Dick again.

Years later I heard he'd been unsuccessful in getting an officer's commission. He refused to be inducted as a private and might have gone to jail with another and tougher Draft Board. However, he was lucky. His Draft Board decided that as a writer maybe he was a little nutty, peculiar, odd. So instead of a 1-A he was flunked out as a 4-F. Exempt from military service.

Years later, still other stories about Dick Wright. He'd changed, the gossip went. As if we don't all change?

The image sharpest in my mind is the night-haunted father guarding his sleeping baby from the faceless demons. . . .

Owen Dodson:

I met Richard Wright when he was living on Grand Avenue in Brooklyn. He had a basement apartment and in the back was a yard. He was learning to grow things then. I think it reminded him of his roamings in the fields and farms of his native Mississippi. At any rate, what is so phenomenal about this particular era was that aside from his writing, he was reading everything he could about raising vegetables, flowers, and all varieties of plants and fruits. This self-imposed learning was part of the psychological pattern of his life. He would spend, say, a year on gardening, and then take up another subject like physics to explore that. In other words, it was self-education, and it filled those hours that were not for creative writing.

A great deal of his charm was the exploration of things he was never able to study. I can say he was one of the warmest, and most generous and gentle writers I have ever met. He was never jealous of someone else's work. He criticized with forthrightness which never had an edge of jealousy to discourage, especially young writers.

He was generous in recommending his publishers to them, and especially urging them to be forthright about the truth of the lives that they lived and saw about. So many times when I was invited to his apartment on Charles Street in the Village, he was surrounded by people who came from various parts of the world and made a special point of visiting him because they so admired what he had done to reveal the life of the Negro . . . and one thing that strikes me now so forcefully is that in all of his work, in spite of the sordid life that he could depict, he was always revealed as if he were a Pilgrim, inquiring the Why and Wherefore, and in his tragedy like *Native Son*, the special appeal and the tragic essence is that Bigger Thomas was ready to live when he was doomed to die. It was not that Bigger Thomas lost the fight or the bitterness, but that he knew that life somehow could be better, in spite of the handicaps, the traps that even angels fell into, and so Bigger died with a large dream that was not the dream of a murderer, but the dream of a man who had been condemned, not because he committed a crime, but because Justice was ignorant of the inner turmoil that a Black Man, yes, any deprived people, must Fight, and Fight, and Fight, and sometimes, overcome. This was his redemption as he held to the bars of his cell during his last heartbreaking hours.

Before he went to Paris, I met at his Charles Street house Simone de Beauvoir (who was the champion), along with Jean Paul Sartre, of Existentialism. This philosophy impressed Dick whole-heartedly, because he knew at the center of every act is not only a cause for that act, but that a kind of redemption can come if the person was willing to face what he had done, mayhem, murder, theft, violent adultery, battery. Richard Wright had true compassion for the people who, in the eyes of society, were criminals and needed help, not from a prison, but from the embracement of brotherhood.

The last time I talked with Richard was over the phone in Paris, and before I could ask him HOW IS IT GOING? HOW ARE YOU DOING?—DO YOU FEEL FREE? . . . WAS IT WORTH LEAVING CHICAGO, NEW YORK, MISSISSIPPI TO BE EMBRACED BY A FOREIGN LAND? . . . before I could ask him those, he said HOW IS YOUR WORK COMING? . . . WHY HAVEN'T YOU SENT ME MORE? . . . WHY HAVEN'T YOU WRITTEN ME? . . . I WOULD LIKE TO SEE YOU . . . He wanted to know what the kids are doing in the world of Art and Letters . . .what the young people are doing to reshape the crooked outlines that were so falsely and ruthlessly drawn to give America her pragmatism.

I would like to speak of his life of Poetry and Little Children, because they are one and the same—at least to me. No matter where he was going, how close the time was to an appointment, he found time to talk to little children along the street, and his gracious and sincere smile would make them talk to him, and I remember Dick best this way . . . the Black Boy who became a man, but never forgot the mystery and wonder of childhood even when he was a great figure.

FRANK K. SAFFORD, M.D. *(as told to Elizabeth Hill Downey)*:

Perhaps you will be interested in what might have been a turning point in Richard Wright's life. Twenty-five years ago I rented a cottage to Dick, his wife Ellen, his first child and a Siamese cat. (There were four cottages, one winterized house on a hill overlooking Long Island Sound and a large beach house available to all tenants.)

Richard was "riding high" at a peak in his popularity still reacting to his published overthrow of allegiance to the Communist Party, disillusioned by Stalinism and intrigued by Existentialism.

With the exception of Horace Cayton, the sociologist from South Side Chicago, and an occasional guest, Richard was the only black resident in a very small and insular village—Wading River, Long Island—where he never seemed defensive because of color. He was, instead, rather affectionate and always ready to parry any argument and was often the life of the party. We had many talk fests with Maurice Hindus, Nat Wolf, John Rothschild (who was partner to James Michener in the "Open Road") and Knox Hall Montgomery, a Technocrat, plus various other stray artists, photographers and intellectuals who drifted in from Yaddo, Greenwich Village and foreign countries.

Wright became attached to our little bit of naturalness and asked me to find him property upon which to build. After what seemed to be normal negotiations, either village pressure and/or prejudice caused the owner to refuse to sell. At the end of the summer season Richard returned to Paris to make it his permanent headquarters as an expatriot. I visited him in Paris in 1952 to find him almost daily involved in more discussions of Existentialism at the Cafe du Maggot.

When in Wading River he was invariably curious about our entire family and the patients who came to recuperate at our large beach house. One of our tenants began to show the early symptoms of Multiple Sclerosis and Richard quizzed me for hours about the disease with many astute and probing questions, admittedly with the idea of using the information in his writing. With rare exception all members of our loosely knit commune felt great warmth to him, with the possible exception of our childrens' nurse, a bible-belt black girl, whom he taunted as being servile—but never with malice, just his usual game of verbal ping pong.

HARRY BIRDOFF:

When I first met Richard Wright, his novel, *Native Son,* was being fashioned into a play during the spring of 1941.

He was a natty dresser. He wore new brown shoes, bright green socks matched by a green tie, and a thin gold watch chain hung across the top of his tweed trousers. He had a pleasant smile, trace of a Southern drawl—a well-modulated, high pitched voice. He did not wear glasses in public, only when writing, I learned later.

During rehearsals one would expect the author to be glued to his seat at the theatre. Actually, Wright attended only three or four times. He confessed that he had not seen a single play on Broadway, and said that he didn't particularly care. The movies were his "dish." When I questioned him, he said, "Because I think peoples' lives are like the movies."

Playwriting was altogether a baffling matter to Wright. He told the following story about himself: while adapting *Native Son* with the help of Paul Green, the latter wanted an excuse to bring someone onto the sidewalk (Scene II, Ernie's Kitchen Shack, in "the gullet of narrow alleyway leading back into the shadows"). Richard Wright was asked what a logical activity would be. "Well," suggested the author, "he could be carrying a pail of water and emptying it into the gutter."

"There's only one trouble with that," said Green. "The first row spectators don't like to get wet."

At the opening performance at the St. James Theatre, March 24th, I noted the play's departure from orthodox staging. There were deep menacing shadows — a tension felt throughout. No playbills were given, nor were there intermissions during the 10 scenes. When Bigger was cornered—"Come out, you black bastard!"—he cowered, firing straight into the audience. Answering shots and searchlights came from the rear of the theatre. Sirens were turned on, increasing in pitch—and the Curtain fell.

Orson Welles, the director, staged the trial scene with the judge facing the audience; they were separated by the railing across the apron of the stage. Below the railing, in the pit, sat the defence attorney, Bigger and family.

If we compare *Native Son* with modern protest plays, one can't help discovering how free from foul language Wright's play is. Yet to everyone's surprise, when it came to the Majestic Theatre, Lee Shubert, operating the chain, ordered *Native Son* to be closed there. Mr. Shubert capitulated when a mass demonstration was planned.

Actually, this brought a windfall to *Native Son.* The play had been losing money, for that week's gross had been $5,000, not $8,000 as had been reported. After 97 performances the run ended in the June heat.

This incident may appear amusing. My sister-in-law, Sara Hibble, was a close friend of Ellen Poplar, whom Richard Wright was courting at the time. During that period the author occupied an old two-family house in Brooklyn, that dated back to Civil War days. It was on Waverly, just off the corner of Fulton Street. When my wife became Wright's secretary, she would describe to me how during dictation her fingers would become numb with cold. Wright would go down into the cellar and stoke the furnace. Often this action recalled to my wife the horrifying scene in the novel: Bigger disposing of Mary's body by stuffing it into the coals! When she mentioned it to Wright, he burst into laughter.

Passersby would stop and stare into Wright's window as my wife sat typing his manuscripts. They either mistook her for his wife, or thought how strange for a white woman to work for a Negro.

Wright attempted at this time what he described as a "sort of feminine-counterpart of *Native Son.*" He spent mornings at a rundown employment agency on lower Fulton Street, near the Brooklyn Bridge. He made copious notes as the migrant colored help were interviewed.

I have since wondered what became of the manuscript, *Black Hope,* a 100 page novelette, with the heroine named "Charity." The theme was suggested by a story in Edward Zeltner's New York *Mirror* column.

It ran something like this: In Brooklyn Heights there was a house that was considered the showplace of the neighborhood. Visitors to that section were always shown the edifice (from the outside). But it was a mystery: no one ever saw the people who lived there. Only the colored servants were on view. For example, every morning a colored chauffeur would walk out the door, get into a shiny car and drive off—alone. The maids would be seen under similar circumstances. Finally it was discovered that these Negroes were the only occupants of the house, and that they pretended to be servants for fear the neighborhood would be up in arms against Negroes living there.

"My own stuff comes pretty slow," Wright confessed to my wife. "There are no fireworks in my life, just work day in and day out." He couldn't write unless it was very quiet; hence his later choice of the sleepy Brooklyn Heights section, where he lived with Ellen, and where their first child, Julia, was born. He called the baby "Sunshine."

Habitually, Wright would sharpen at least fifty pencils to the minutest point imaginable before my wife arrived each afternoon. He dictated from the "Rough." There were usually four typewritten drafts before his manuscripts were completed. The lines were triple-spaced, with an immense margin on both sides, on paper long as galley-proof sheets. He edited and polished and cut. I once met him in the subway, where he sat revising a next-to-the-last draft that he carried in a loose-leaf notebook.

This is an example of his revision: In *12 Million Black Voices,* his most lyrical work, I noted curiously that the first draft bore this description of how the early slaves were tied up and transported: "like spoons laid out in the holds of the ships." In the final revision the cliché was removed, and became "stacked up like cord-wood in the foul holes of clipper ships."

The advent of World War II made publication rather problematical, with the shortage of paper, but Richard Wright did try to find a publisher for my *World's Greatest Hit.*

In a letter (Dec. 17, 1941) he said, "As a Negro, naturally I am concerned about how the greatest folk play of my race was received over the world." His first book was called *Uncle Tom's Children.* Once I mentioned to him that Universal Pictures had filmed *Uncle Tom's Cabin* using a noted old side-wheeler, "Kate Adams," on the Mississippi, and how a few weeks later an explosion and fire had burnt her to the water's edge. Wright recalled that as a boy he had sailed on her, and that it was a sensation that remained with him. He described it in *Black Boy.*

The last time I saw Richard Wright was in 1947. Soon after an eight-month stay in France, he bought a three-story brick house on Charles Street in Greenwich Village. I was surprised to run into him, one day, on Fulton Street. In his late thirties, scholarly-looking, he was casually dressed in putty-gray slacks, brown shirt, tan jacket and apricot-colored tie. His voice was clear and light, and his laugh was almost child-like. I asked what he was doing in this black-ghetto section of Brooklyn. He answered that he was accepted as a writer in Greenwich Village, but that he could not get a hair-cut there.

KING JOE

(JOE LOUIS BLUES)

Recorded on Okeh Record No. 6475

By PAUL ROBESON and COUNT BASIE and his Orchestra

Lyric by
RICHARD WRIGHT

Music by
COUNT BASIE

Slow Blues Tempo
f
E♭
mf-f
Black-eyed peas ask corn-bread, "What make you so strong?"
Joe don't talk much, but he talks all the time.
E♭7
A♭
E♭
Black-eyed peas ask corn-bread, "What make you so strong?"
Say old Joe don't talk much, he talks all the time.
E♮dim
B♭7 B♭dim B♭7 B♭dim
Fm7 B♮7 B♭+ Fm7
Corn-bread say "I came from where Joe Louis was born."
Now you can look at Joe but you sure don't read his mind.

448 - 3

E♭
Lord, I know a se - cret, swore I'd nev - er tell.
Rab - bit say to bee, what make you sting so deep?
E♭7 A♭ A♭7
Lord I know a se - cret, swore I'd nev - er
Rab - bit say to bee, "what make you sting so
E♭ E♮dim B♭7 B♭dim B♭7 G♭7
tell.
deep?"
I know what makes old Joe hook and
Bee say I sting like Joe and
Fm7 B♮7 B♭7+ Fm7 E♭ Fm7
punch and roll like hell.
rock 'em all to sleep.
They say old
Been in

Eb
Eb7
Joe just lays down sleeps — all day long; —
Cleve-land, St. Louis, and Chi - ca - go too; —
They say old
Been in
Ab
Ab
Eb
Joe just lays down sleeps — all day long; —
Cleve - land, St. Louis and Chi - ca - go too; —
Ebdim
Bb7
Bbdim
Bb7
Bbdim
Fm7
Bb7
Bb+
Fm7
What old Joe does at night Lord, sure aint done him no
But the best is Har - lem when a Joe Louis fight is
1. Eb
Fm7
2. Eb
wrong —
They say
through —

ADDITIONAL LYRICS

KING JOE

(JOE LOUIS BLUES)

Lyrics by **RICHARD WRIGHT** *Music by* **COUNT BASIE**

Old Joe wrestled Ford engines, Lord, it was a shame;
Say old Joe hugged Ford engines, Lord, it was a shame;
And he turned engine himself and went to the fighting game.

If you want to see something, just watch Old Joe roll with a blow,
If you want to see something, just watch Old Joe roll with a blow,
Lord, Lord, bet he didn't learn that trick at no boxing show.

Big Black bearcat couldn't turn nothing loose he caught;
Big Black bearcat couldn't turn nothing loose he caught;
Squeezed it 'til the count of nine, and just couldn't be bought.

Now molasses is black and they say buttermilk is white,
Now molasses is black and they say buttermilk is white,
If you eat a bellyful of both, it's like a Joe Louis fight.

Wonder what Joe Louis thinks when he's fighting a white man,
Say wonder what Joe thinks when he's fighting a white man?
Bet he thinks what I'm thinking, 'cause he wears a deadpan.

Lord, I hate to see old Joe Louis step down,
Lord, I hate to see old Joe Louis step down,
But I bet a million dollars no man will ever wear his crown.

Bullfrog told boll weevil; Joe's done quit the ring,
Bullfrog told boll weevil; Joe's done quit the ring,
Boll weevil say; He ain't gone and he's still the king.

Native Son On Stage

John Houseman

Among the books that were sent up to us in our retreat at Victorville, where Herman Mankiewicz and I were working on the script of *Citizen Kane,* was Richard Wright's *Native Son.* We both read it and decided immediately that we should adapt it to the stage. Having learned that Wright was in Mexico, I asked a visiting friend to call upon him and stake our claim. She found him by the side of a pool in Cuernavaca and learned that arrangements had already been made for Paul Green to dramatize the work. I was disappointed, but it was a reasonable choice: Green was the first white playwright to write sympathetically of Negro life in the South. (We had done two of his one-acters as exercises with the Negro Theatre in Harlem and *In Abraham's Bosom,* starring Rose McLendon, had won a Pulitzer prize in 1927. More recently *Evenin' Sun Go Down* had been done on the same New Theatre night as Odets' *Waiting for Lefty.*) I had my own personal doubts as to Green's suitability for the task: *Native Son* was a violent, revolutionary work that did not accord with Green's perceptive and sensitive but essentially Southern, rural attitude toward the race problem in America. (My doubts would have been even graver if I had known of Green's attitude as reflected in the three "stipulations" which he described years later to the editor of *Black Drama*—"one being that I would have freedom to invent new characters and make editorial story changes where necessary, another being that I could make the Communist slant in the book comic when I felt like it." The third was that, though Wright would not be writing any of the dramatization, he would "come and be with me during my dramatizing work—this last being necessary for discussion purposes as I went along.") However, it was done, and the next best thing was to try and secure the producing rights. With my record in the Negro Theatre this was not difficult, and, in July,

Paul Reynolds informed me that Wright was returning from Mexico and would go directly to North Carolina to work with Paul Green on the play script.

I was there when Wright arrived—a surprisingly mild-mannered, round-faced, brown-skinned young man with beautiful eyes. It was only later, when I came to know him better, that I began to sense the deep, almost morbid violence that lay skin-deep below that gentle surface. At that first meeting I was surprised — not altogether agreeably, having read his books—by the blandness with which he recounted the shameful story of his return to his native land. At Brownsville, at the border, a Texan customs inspector had pawed through his baggage, suspiciously examined and criticized his manuscripts and books ("Where's your Bible, boy?") and demanded to know where he got the money for travel and clothes. On the train that carried him across the South he had, of course, been denied access to the dining car, and the black waiter carrying his meal to the Jim Crow chair car had been stopped as he passed through the train and forbidden to serve a nigger on dining-car china with white men's linen and silver.

I spent a day with him and Green, listening to Paul's ideas for the play. I watched Dick Wright for his reactions: I saw nothing. But my own apprehensions rose sharply. Paul Green was a man who sincerely believed himself free of racial prejudice. His action in inviting Wright to live in his home during their collaboration was an act of some courage—even in an academic community like Chapel Hill. Throughout his stay, according to Dick, he could not have been more courteous, thoughtful and hospitable in his treatment of his black guest. But having granted him social equality, he stopped. From the first hour of their "discussions" it became clear that he was incapable or unwilling to extend this equality into the professional or creative fields. Whether from his exalted position as veteran playwright and Pulitzer prize-winner or from some innate sense of intellectual and moral superiority (aggravated by Wright's Communist connections), Paul Green's attitude in the collaboration was, first and last, insensitive, condescending and intransigent. No less disturbed than Wright by the injustices and cruelties of the racial situation in America, he was in total disagreement with him as to its solution. The basic and radical premise of Wright's novel—that only through an act of violence could a Negro like Bigger Thomas break through the massive and highly organized repressive structure by which he was surrounded ("The most I could say of Bigger was that he felt the *need* for a whole life and *acted* out that need; that was all") was something that Green absolutely refused to accept—morally or artistically. Resenting what he called Dick's existentialism, he attempted, till the day of the play's opening—through madness, reprieve, suicide, regeneration and other "purging" and sublimating devices—to evade and dilute the dramatic conclusion with which Wright had consciously and deliberately ended a book in which he wanted his readers to face the horrible truth "without the consolation of tears."

When I left them to their uneasy collaboration, Green estimated it would take him less than two months for a first draft. Until then there was nothing I could do but tamp down my apprehensions and start making arrangements for an early production, so as to profit from *Native Son*'s continued presence on the best-seller lists. I called Mankiewicz to tell him of my progress. Instead, I had to listen to his ambivalent ravings about "Monstro" (his latest name for Welles) whom he alternately described as (1) A genius shooting one of the greatest films ever made. (2) A scoundrel and a thief who was now claiming sole credit for the writing of *Citizen Kane.* Infected by his indignation, I sat down and wrote a letter to Orson in which I informed him that if anyone but Mank was to get credit for the script of *Kane* it would be me, and that I was prepared to enforce my claim through the Screen Writers' Guild on the basis of my writer's contract with Mercury Productions. The next morning I tore the letter up.

Five or six weeks later I got a call from Richard in North Carolina saying that Green's first draft had gone to the typist and that he would be returning to New York. I asked him to wait till I had a chance to read it, but he said there was nothing more he could do. He sounded so discouraged that I told him I would be down the next day and drive him back. Knowing my mother's passion for motoring, I invited her to drive with me through country she had never seen. We arrived in Chapel Hill at night, and the next morning I met with Wright and Green, who seemed satisfied with his work. Richard said nothing, but on the way up I sensed enough to ask him with some impatience why, if he was so disturbed, he had not spoken up and given me a chance to provoke a confrontation. Wright, who had quit the Party but remained a disciplined Marxist, replied that under no circumstances would he risk a public disagreement with a man like Paul Green. There were too many people on both sides anxious to enjoy a dogfight between a successful black intellectual and a white Southern writer of progressive reputation—an avowed "friend" of the Negro people.

It was getting dark when we reached Washington, D.C. We had agreed to go on through to New York, but we were famished and we decided, now that we were out of the South, to stop for something to eat. We parked the car on an avenue facing the White House and the three of us went into a cafeteria on the corner which, at that hour, was almost empty. We had served ourselves and were about to sit down when the manager came up and informed us quietly but firmly that no colored were allowed. I asked him if that was the law. He said it was. I began to yell at him: in that case why had my friend been allowed to serve himself? He said that was a mistake and he was sorry. I asked where we were to eat the food we had paid for. He said he would gladly take back my friend's food and refund the money. I refused. My mother had begun to express her cosmopolitan views on racial equality when Dick, who had not said a word, started for the exit with his tray and we followed him. It was a warm night, and the three of us sat on the curb and ate our supper while Dick explained to my mother that he was accustomed to this sort of thing which would never change until the entire system was changed. We left our trays on the sidewalk when we were finished and as we got back into the car and headed North, we saw the man from the cafeteria picking them up.

Some days later a "first rough working draft" arrived—a hundred and forty pages long. Structurally it stayed fairly close to the book, which Wright had consciously written in dramatic scene form ("I wanted the reader to feel that Bigger's story was happening *now* like a play upon a stage or a movie on a screen.") But the "editorial changes"—the additions and modifications—exasperated me. Among the former was a wholly invented, Dostoievskian police "reenactment" scene for which I saw no necessity in a script that was already overlong. Among the modifications was the blending of the dead girl's Communist boyfriend with the left-wing labor lawyer who finally undertakes Bigger's defence. Even more serious in my opinion was the changed moral attitude that pervaded the script, leading inevitably to a total betrayal of Wright's intention in the closing scene. This was the scene of which Wright had written:

> At last I found how to end the book; I ended it just as I had begun it, showing Bigger living dangerously, taking his life in his hands, accepting what life had made of him. The lawyer, Max, was placed in Bigger's cell at the end to register the moral—or what I felt was the moral—horror of Negro life in the United States.

This final facing of the terrible truth of his life was distorted, in Green's version, by giving Bigger "lyric" delusions of grandeur in which he saw himself as "a black God, single and alone."

> BIGGER
>
> Ring the bells! Beat the gongs! Put my name on the hot wires of the world—the name of Bigger, Bigger—the man who walked with God—walked this earth like God—was God!

During the final fade-out a priest in a white surplice "with a great book in his hand" intoned *"I am the Resurrection and the Life."*

I called Wright as soon as I had read it and told him of my anger. He asked me to call or write to Paul Green and explain how I felt and why. I tried, and it was like talking to a stone wall. Some weeks later a revised script arrived. It was down to reasonable length; the Dostoievskian reenactment was gone and the laywer, Boris Max (rechristened Paul), had been restored to life. But the basic flaw—the distortion of Wright's book—remained. In his final moments in the death cell, Bigger now burbled of the watermelon-patch back home until "the murmuring throb of an airplane motor" offstage caused "his voice to burst from him in a wild, frenzied call"—

BIGGER

Fly them planes boys — fly 'em! Riding through — riding through. I'll be with you! I'll—

GUARD

He's going nuts.

BIGGER

(Yelling his head wagging in desperation)

Keep on driving! To the end of the world—Smack into the face of the sun!

(Gasping)

Fly 'em for me—for Bigger—

(The sound of the airplane fades away and now the death chant of the prisoners comes more loudly into the scene. In the dim corridor at the rear, the white surplice of a priest is discerned . . . They start leading him from the cell. As of its own volition the door to the little death house opens and a flood of light pours out. Bigger with his eyes set and his shoulders straight, moves toward its sunny radiance like a man walking into a deep current of water. The guards quietly follow him, their heads bent down.)

PRIEST'S VOICE

(Intoning from the shadows)

I am the resurrection and the light.

THE END

I urged Wright to repudiate what I considered a deliberate betrayal of his work. I told him I had no intention of producing the play in its present form. Dick continued to be distressed but repeated that he preferred not to see it produced than to risk a public disagreement with Paul Green at this time. There was nothing more I could do. My option ran for three and a half months longer. I put the script away in a drawer, swallowed my disappointment and turned back to other work.

Then one morning, shortly before Thanksgiving, I awoke in my raised red-velvet bed and raged at the thought that I owned one of the hottest theatrical properties in the world and was prevented from doing anything with it by a peculiar combination of Southern moral prejudice and black, Marxist scruples. I called up Dick Wright and asked him to come over to Ninth Street for lunch. I assured him that I understood those scruples but that as his producer and director I refused to accept them. I had re-examined the book and Green's dramatization of it: the revised version was structurally sound; wherever it followed the novel it was usable; where it deviated, as in the absurd final scene, it was reparable by returning to his own original text. Dick asked if we would let Green know what we were doing. I said no. I wanted Wright's help in the restoration, but it would be done entirely on my authority as producer and I would assume full responsibility for it.

Almost every morning, for three weeks, he came over from Brooklyn and we would work our way through the scenes, transfusing the blood of the novel back into the body of the play. We had a good time, and when we were done I had the script retyped and took it with me to California, where I was flown at the invitation of David Selznick, who was looking for an associate producer to help run his studio while he rested after his triumphs with *Gone With The Wind* and *Rebecca.* I listened to him talk for four hours, then drove to RKO, where Orson ran the work print of *Citizen Kane* for me. That night, in my first spasm of enthusiasm, I did what I had vowed I would never do again. Over dinner I gave Orson the new script of *Native Son* and asked him if he would like to direct it as a Mercury production.

He called me in New York two days later and said yes, very much, as soon as he had seen *Citizen Kane* through its releasing pains—probably in mid-February. My feelings were mixed by this time. I had set my heart on directing this one myself. But I was anxious to end my theatrical association with Welles on a note of triumph and I felt that with the strong text of Wright's book to support him, his direction of *Native Son* would be more dramatic than mine. I gave Wright the news and he was delighted. So was Paul Green.

Meantime I found myself unexpectedly involved in a curious venture with, of all people, the Theatre Guild. Once again Lawrence Langner and Theresa Helburn had to suffer my hateful presence—this time at the insistence of Philip Barry, who, with *The Philadelphia Story,* had become the most successful playwright and could not be denied.

The play he wanted me to direct for him was a variation of a script he had given me to read two years earlier under the title *The Wild Harps Playing.* It was a frail, whimsical, vaguely poetic piece (a love child among his more mundane commercial plays) about the final, visionary hours of a poor little rich Irish girl dying of a mysterious, incurable ailment. He had laid it aside when he could not get it produced, then returned to it after the huge success of *The Philadelphia Story* and tried to fortify it with elements of contemporary political significance. He rechristened his heiress *Liberty Jones* and related her decline to the presence of three villainous figures who were clearly identifiable as the three totalitarian powers. From their unholy conspiracy she was saved by an upstanding juvenile who vaguely suggested the United States of America. In the process of change it had become a flimsy musical with songs and ballets. This is what finally induced me to undertake it. Raoul Pène duBois did the sets and costumes and as choreographer and principal dancer I used Lew Christiansen, who had done *Filling Station* with us the year before. With every ingénue in New York competing for the role of Liberty Jones, Nancy Coleman won out by a nose over Dorothy McGuire, who, brokenhearted, accepted the name part in *Claudia* across the street and became a star overnight.

I had as good a time as I could with a production that I was directing without real conviction or hope of success. We went through the usual stages of nervousness in New Haven, made the usual meaningless changes and played to Guild subscribers in Philadelphia and then in New York without arousing either indignation or enthusiasm. The critics were mild but kind and *Liberty Jones* was still running when *Native Son* went into rehearsal late in February.

Citizen Kane had barely survived Hearst's attempts to torpedo it. It received generally brilliant reviews but no major theatre chain was willing to show it; it was not until some years later that it was universally accepted as the masterpiece that it is.

My relationship with Orson was quite different now from what it had been during our partnership, but this made it easier for us to be together. Throughout rehearsals of *Native Son* he was happy, overbearing and exciting to work with. With Jean Rosenthal (who was beginning to make her reputation on the outside) and, once again, Jimmy Morcom (on leave from Radio City), we worked out a production in which, behind a vast permanent brick-painted portal, ten wagon stages of various sizes moved past and around each other with never more than a few inches to spare. It took thirty-five stagehands to move them but they worked without a hitch. And for once I had no money problems. Since *Kane,* Hollywood was suddenly full of operators eager for a piece of the action—Orson's action. Two of them, in the hope of becoming his partners in future film ventures, put up the money for *Native Son* to the tune of fifty-five thousand dollars.

Casting was a pleasure. The Mercury regulars—those who had not stayed in California after *Citizen Kane*—were reassembled: Ray Collins (who played Max, the lawyer), Everett Sloane, Paul Stewart, Erskine Sanford, Jack Berry and others. New faces included Philip Bourneuf from the Federal Theatre, Frances Bavier, Joseph Pevney and Anne Burr, a complete unknown chosen in an open audition, as the girl. For our black actors we turned to old friends from the Lafayette: Evelyn Ellis, Helen Martin, Rena Mitchell, Bootsie Davis, Wardell Saunders and Canada Lee, a former prize fighter and night-club owner who had played Banquo for us in *Macbeth* and whom the role of Bigger Thomas made a Broadway star.

For our script we used the text Wright and I had worked on: the few changes we made in rehearsal were all returns to the book. Dick came regularly and appeared to enjoy himself. Then one day I got word that Paul Green would be in New York for the final run-throughs. He appeared in the theatre one evening, sat in silence and left without a word after the last scene. The next morning, the day of our first preview, we held a meeting: Green, Wright, Paul Reynolds and I, joined by Welles, who was rehearsing downstairs and whom I summoned at a dramatic moment. Green insisted that we reinstate his version—particularly the final scene. I told him it was much too late for that and, besides, we had no intention of being parties to the distortion of a work we admired. Richard sat silent beside his agent, who now informed us that Green's second draft (credited to Paul Green and Richard Wright) was already in the publisher's hands. I suggested to Green that he get it back and change it to conform to the acting version. Green was furious. There was talk of enjoining the performance, which I knew he could not do, all the more since not one word was spoken on that stage that was not Wright's—particularly in the last scene, where we had gone back word for word to the book. When Orson began to howl at him, Green got up and left, and I have never seen him again. After our successful opening I called his publisher and pointed out the absurdity of the situation. But it was too late to do anything about it, and as long as it remained in print, Harper and Bros. continued to circulate a version of the play that was radically different from what had been performed on the stage of the St. James Theatre.

At the final preview of *Native Son* two sets of pickets appeared on 44th Street. One, from the conservative Urban League, was protesting the squalor of the book and the bad light in which it put the Negro people. The other represented a small, purist faction of the American Communist Party, which could not forgive Richard Wright for having defied Party orders and refused to rewrite certain sections of his book at their behest. They left after an hour and did not reappear on opening night, which took place on the night of March 24 as a Mercury Production presented by Orson Welles and John Houseman.

> Mr. Wright and Paul Green have written a powerful drama and Orson Welles has staged it with imagination and force. These are the first things to be said about the overwhelming play that opened at the St. James last evening but they hardly convey the excitement of this first performance of

> a play that represents experience of life and conviction in thought and a production that represents a dynamic use of the stage.

This from *The New York Times.* Approval came from widely different quarters—for Canada Lee, for Welles and for the production. Burns Mantle in the *Daily News* gave us four stars and was impressed by the "symphonic binder of sound" (an improved variant of our ill-fated street noises in *Julius Caesar)* that held the multiple scenes of our intermissionless show together. The *Christian Science Monitor* approved. The *Daily Worker* enthused.

> In comparison, all the productions of the current season seem dim and ancient chromos. The theatre, that slumbering giant, tears off its chains in this production. From the theatrical point of view it is a technical masterpiece. As a political document it lives with the fire of an angry message.

Stark Young found Canada Lee's performance the best he had ever seen from a Negro player.

> *Native Son* also gains by the thunderous and lurid theatre methods of Mr. Welles. In my opinion Mr. Welles is one of the best influences our theatre has, one of its most important forces . . . His talent begins with the violent, the abundant and the inspired-obvious, all of which make for the life of the theatre-art as contrasted with the pussyfooting and the pseudo-intelligence and the feminism that has crept into this theatre of ours.

What reservations there were came mostly from those whose admiration for the book led them to question the wisdom of dramatizing it:

> In trying to bring *Native Son* to the stage the Mercury has done better than might be expected with the impossible . . . The production achieves something and the almost unbearable suspense of Wright's novel. (John Mason Brown in the New York *Post.)*
>
> *Native Son* is a vivid evening in the theatre, a tragic case of a morally mangled victim of society and circumstance. All the same the play lacks the richness and subterraneous power of the book as well as its essential meaning. We do not get the novel's down-pressing, unanswerable

charge against the white race for crushing and crippling the black one. (Louis Kronenberger in *P.M.)*

The critic of the *Journal American,* loyal to his angry master, William Randolph Hearst, detected "propaganda that seems nearer to Moscow than Harlem" and reminded readers that Richard Wright had been a staff member of the *Daily Worker* and the *New Masses* and had approved the Soviet trials. "It may be that his idea of justice has been warped to acquit Party members of any charge but execute everybody else."

Native Son was a hit and did excellent business. It needed to, for with its large cast and three dozen stagehands it was as expensive to run as a musical. After 114 performances, with the coming of the hot weather, Orson's Hollywood backers decided to close it. (It reopened in the fall in a more economical version that played New York, Chicago, and major Eastern cities for the better part of a year.) By then Welles and I were both living in California: Orson preparing *The Magnificent Ambersons* and I as vice-president of David O. Selznick Productions.

I was on the Coast when I received a note, forwarded from Ninth Street:

Dear John Houseman:

I am sorry that we did not get a chance to have a drink and a talk a little before you left for Hollywood . . .

The object of this letter is to try to express to you my gratitude for the enormous help you gave me with *Native Son.* If it had not been for your willingness to give so generously of your time, I doubt gravely if *Native Son* would have ever seen the boards of Broadway. It was a little shameful and ridiculous that you could not have gotten public credit for that help, but that would have meant my dragging into the open those all-too-touchy relations between Paul Green and me, and I was seeking, above all, to keep any word of dissension out of the public press.

I enjoyed immensely working with you, and if our days in this world are long enough, perhaps we shall meet again under more favorable circumstances.

Give my regards to your mother.

As ever,
Dick Wright

Native Son in the Movies

THOMAS CRIPPS

"He confessed that he had not seen a single play on Broadway, and said that he didn't particularly care. The movies were his 'dish'. When I questioned him, he said, 'Because I think peoples' lives are like the movies.' "—Harry Birdoff

Richard Wright reared back, his dimpled brown face broken with gasping, shrill laughter. Harold Hecht, a Hollywood producer, had just written him a proposal to adapt for the screen Wright's famous novel, *Native Son.* The ludicrous part of the offer was Hecht's wish to make Bigger Thomas, the black anti-hero, into a white man. He was to be part of a circular structure along with a Negro and a Jew who step aside and let Bigger have a job they all wanted. "At the end of the picture," wrote Hecht:

> We will tie this together by a scene with the Jew and the Negro who realize that it could have happened to them, or to anyone who does not have the opportunity of living in equality with other people; that when one group is disenfranchised the meaning and the basis of what we live for is destroyed.

The quotation is from Constance Webb's *Richard Wright* (New York, 1968) which is the most reliable book of the slim literature on Wright (because of its closeness to his papers and memoirs), and the work upon which one must depend for the details of his life. But the comic moment could not cover Wright's mixed anxiety and desire to make a movie. Wright and other Negro intellectuals were like moths around a flame, suspicious and fearful of Hollywood, yet flitting toward the unfulfilled black dream of making a motion picture that truly spoke for blacks and redeemed the medium from its long history of demeaning images.

Richard Wright was Bigger Thomas. Hollywood was his Mary Dalton, holding out the promise of glamor and celebrity for a noble primitive who could write. In an early foreshadowing of his eventual lethal contact with the white world Bigger sits through a pulpy Hollywood double feature, *The Gay Woman and Trader Horn,* in a grind house. It is the white world, remote and inaccessible, set before him, and set against the drums and shouts of the black. By way of contrast, in Walker Percy's *The Moviegoer* the fey white hero is given support for both his temporal and fantasy lives. The way some remember a touching childhood incident, he recalls the way John Wayne shot it out in the street with Luke Plummer in *Stagecoach.* Bigger knows too much. Even if he shot it out surely he would stand alone and guilty, the white authorities uncomprehending and outraged, rather than winking their approval at Wayne who rides off to Mexico with Anne Baxter.

Wright was the latest in the long line of blacks who thought of the cinema as a logical extension of their work, and like them he suffered defeat at its hands. *Native Son* was an immediate artistic and commercial success upon its publication in 1940, and Hollywood producers saw it as a potential motion picture. For the next few years Wright's interest in movies slowly grew from initial contempt to a driving demiurge to score a cinema hit that would match the literary success of his most celebrated novel. His failure marks another dry well along with those of Booker T. Washington, Oscar Micheaux, Paul Robeson, Wallace Thurman, Charles Gilpin, and more recently, Gordon Parks and Melvin Van Peebles, in the long search for a means to crack the most formidable of white institutional expressions. Lack of experience, of capital, of access to distribution, of technicians, of press agentry that could touch minds of both blacks and whites all contributed to the failure of blacks in the cinema. If film had been as cheap as paper and typewriter ribbon, and movies had been sold by the copy like books, perhaps black moviemakers would have swelled in numbers along with the scores of black writers. But movies represented an ephemeral prize awarded to those with a flair for working in an expensive, overorganized, cutthroat, frenetic, collective art-as-industry. Few blacks, especially among the intellectuals, had access to the requisite money and experience. White segregation and the black culture created to survive it conspired to seal off Hollywood from blacks as surely as Watts was isolated by its inefficient bus service.

Wright decided in 1948 to go it alone and make his own movie, ignorant of the failures of others. Booker T. Washington had died in 1915 on the eve of production of a nightmarish black rebuttal to D. W. Griffith's offensive *Birth of a Nation.* Paul Robeson's cinema career was marked by remorse at what Hollywood made him do, and regret at the lost opportunities and misfired attempts elsewhere. Robeson had lucklessly tried every avenue: an Oscar Micheaux' "race picture," *Body and Soul* in 1924; Kenneth Macpherson's unreleased experiment, *Borderline*, in 1929; Dudley Murphy's version of *Emperor Jones*, shot on Long Island; and his series of British movies with Zoltan Korda and others. Micheaux, through a quarter of a century of all-black movies outside of Hollywood circles, could never find the artistic glimmer to go with his driving energy and perseverance. Wallace Thurman came to Hollywood from his New York hit, *Harlem*, and died before he could develop his craft. Charles Gilpin, thought to be the finest Negro actor of his day, died from hard drinking and rage at Hollywood's demands on him during his tenure in Universal's *Uncle Tom's Cabin* in 1926. Parks and Van Peebles have combined their art with varying degrees of independence from studios as they still move toward the elusive black statement in a white world.

Like Bigger's confrontation with the glitter of white society that contrasted with his own squalor, Wright's meeting with Hollywood also threatened his existence and his art. Although Wright at first laughed at Hollywood's naïve overtures, he willingly wasted three years in Argentina through the tedium and disappointments of putting together a bad movie, as he tried to use the larger-than-life mythical quality of movies to stretch his reach to a new audience. As surely as Bigger groped for some real contact with Mary Dalton, the white girl whom he accidentally kills, Wright wanted movies to speak to blacks and whites in ways he could not achieve in the novel form. And as surely as Mary must die and pull Bigger after her, the movie industry must strangle the life from Wright's literary work. And just as Bigger stupidly aids his tormentors, Wright, through ignorance, vanity, and finally abdication of his responsibility for the final release-print, contributed to making his powerful novel into a stumbling movie.

His first brush with Hollywood was innocuous enough. In 1940 during the first flush of success of *Native Son* he was invited to do a screenplay from Booker T. Washington's autobiography. The second contact came soon after in Mexico where Wright fled to escape the jangle of literary fame, Book-of-the-Month selection, appointment to the New York World's Fair Hall of Fame, the requests of chic magazine editors, the temptation to wallow in the thick stream of fatuous praise flowing from middle brow magazines. Irene Lee of Warner Brothers came down to Cuernavaca to discuss a Broadway production of *Native Son* and an eventual film, both to be shaped by the contribution of Orson Welles, fresh from *Citizen Kane.* But Wright's marriage was crumbling and he fled Mexico as quickly as he had decided to escape New York. He meandered through his Southern home grounds and then on to Chicago and finally to Chapel Hill, North Carolina, where he at last met Welles and Paul Green, the playwright whom Wright chose to adapt *Native Son* for the stage under the aegis of Welles' Mercury Theatre. They put the play on the boards; but war intervened and the possible movie engaged Wright only fitfully until 1948.

In the years between 1940 and 1948 white producers demanded changes in Wright's work, so much so that the refusals should have honed Wright's ability to resist diluting his work. From the left and from the right well-meaning critics had attacked the ideological foundations of his work. Even before Wright dropped out of the Communist Party its leaders had carped at Bigger's dullness and cowardice, and his bourgeois individualism that ignored the masses. Hollywoodians, on the other hand, were happy that Bigger did not carry all the caste marks of the proletarian hero, but they wished to excise Wright's politics anyway. In fact the two political extremes struggled for control of Hollywood. But his eagerness pushed him closer to the industry and during the war years he wrote a couple of scenarios while he listened to the offers.

In April, 1944, he wrote *Melody Unlimited*, a script about the touring Fisk Jubilee Singers, but no one would buy it. Then, at the request of Eve Ettinger, Columbia's story editor, he and George Crosby collaborated on a script about an American Nazi who worked for the Germans as a broadcaster. Each time, the studio shelved the project. The most serious Hollywood offer seemed the most ludicrous: Harold Hecht's proposal to change Bigger to white. Canada Lee and Mark Miller, who had worked with John Steinbeck on his movie, *The Forgotten Village*, also attempted a film version of the play that Lee had appeared in as Bigger. Unfortunately, Lee took on more Hollywood commitments, eventually dying after a vigorous role as a boxer; Miller failed to discover an "angel;" and worst of all, they decided their English-French version would not sell unless Wright removed its political sting and substituted "non-political disaffiliated humanitarian motivations." Another producer wanted to make a musical of the novel! Wright could only ask with mock candor: "Can you see Bigger Thomas being dragged down the steps to the tune of the 'Surrey With the Fringe on Top?'" The cinema work he really wished to do at the Canadian Film Board was prevented by the director, John Grierson, who thought his abandoning fiction "would be a terrible loss."

Micheaux, or Robeson, or any Negro who had wrestled with the motion picture industry could have warned Wright of the attempts to profit from *Native Son* by removing its sting. The motives for writing a novel were different from those for making a movie and the difference was that between art and profit. In publishing, the two goals were separated by a division of labor; in Hollywood they were joined in the person of the producer. But a black man from Mississippi and the Black Belt of Chicago was not likely to know the difference.

In the summer of 1948 Wright, living in exile in Paris, received a telephone call from Pierre Chenal, a French motion picture director. Curious and excited, Wright arranged to meet him in a cafe. There Wright was taken in by the bubbling and charming Frenchman who had just returned from Argentina where he had seen Paul Green's stage version of *Native Son.* "I must make this film," he said amidst a flurry of gestures.

To Wright his enthusiasm could only mean that at last the novel could be filmed without diluting its powerful indictment of white American society. The years of feeling vaguely uncomfortable in the glare of popularity that seemed to ignore the dark message of his novel seemed at an end. Moreover, Chenal, and his Uruguayan partner, James Prades, both astonished Wright by proposing that the author himself enact his leading character. Together they would share the labor: Prades as producer; Chenal as director-scenarist; Wright as dialogue writer, actor, and guiding light.

From the beginning problems mounted but Wright allowed excitement to mask them. He could not surrender rights because he held them jointly with Paul Green. The partners could not pay for rights except in unstable francs. Also, even though his friends suspected there was bad blood between them, if Wright's screentest proved inadequate, he wanted Canada Lee for the role. While lounging in LeRoy Haynes' soul food restaurant in Paris, Wright fretted over his middle-aged fat and wondered whether he could shed enough of it to look the part of the young, pinched Bigger. Operating separately, Wright bought the rights from Green while Prades and Chenal scraped together more money. The best they could do was a deal for fifty percent of the profits, the rest to be divided three ways. Within a year, the company folded and was replaced by Sono, an Argentine firm. In August, 1949, they sailed for New York, with the worst to come.

That would be Pierre Chenal, the director who had drifted in and out of France and Latin America, making undistinguished films that occasionally caught the eye of some leftist critic. Wright, captured by Chenal's enthusiasm and his flattering interest in the novel, failed to examine his movies, and thereby fell victim to the glib praise that passed for discussion among moviemakers. Wright accepted his reputation and integrity on faith even though his credentials were slim. He had started out writing in documentary films in the silent era and plodded through a humdrum career marked by an occasional interesting piece such as his treatment of Dostoievski's *Crime and Punishment* which the English filmmaker, Paul Rotha, found "passible;" and his adaptation of James M. Cain's *The Postman Always Rings Twice.* Praise for the former may have stemmed from its approval by chic French Leftist intellectuals. Many years later Georges Sadoul, one of France's most distinguished film critics, could find him no more than an overrated hack with "une carrière internationale médiocre." Sadoul's *Histoire du Cinema* and Roy Armes' *French Cinema Since 1946* mention him not at all, while Rene Jeanne and Charles Ford's *Histoire Illustrée du Cinéma* gives him a friendly nod.

But Wright had a bad case of movie fever and he overlooked every flaw in the project. Like Bigger, he became entangled in an alien world that eventually thwarted his ambitions. Isolated from black roots, exiled in Paris, unable to turn to old friends, Wright missed the grinding changes in Hollywood that he might have helped accelerate. Throughout the war years Walter White and the National Association for the Advancement of Colored People had successfully invaded Hollywood after years of campaigning for censorship of odious racial themes. In the early 1940's White arranged a meeting with Darryl Zanuck; the defeated presidential candidate, Wendell Willkie; and others to hammer out a policy for wartime racial change in Hollywood. The result was splashy and very impressive to the Negro press. The major studios began to include important black characters in their war movies: Fox's *Crash Dive* included a rough model of Dorie Miller, the black steward who died at Pearl Harbor; Columbia's *Sahara* featured Rex Ingram as an important Senegalese soldier in the fight against racism and fascism; MGM's *Bataan* placed a black soldier played by Kenneth Spencer among the trapped defenders of the Philippines.

When Wright and Chenal reached New York in the summer of 1949, the pace picked up as they busied themselves with preproduction chores, shaping the shooting script, casting most of the American actors, and giving them copies of the novel. In the early autumn they moved on to Chicago, where they shot exteriors, and then to Buenos Aires where Wright began to have doubts. He and Prades quarreled over the contract, which had been drawn up in hazy Spanish. At every turn they were spied upon, their mail opened and cables intercepted, their shooting interrupted by soldiers, and their taxes and bribes inflated. Deep into the shooting schedule Wright discovered that Prades had lied to their "angel" about costs and scheduling. The morass of deception and bungling scared Prades, so Wright went to their backer and convinced him to sign a new contract taking twenty percent of the gross and excluding Chenal and Prades. The only bright spot was Jean Wallace, the sexy, blue-eyed blonde starlet whose only professional distinction up to then had been her overly public marriage to actor Franchot Tone. Wright liked her intelligence, her sexiness which he liked to kid, her courage in taking a role that would surely get her blacklisted in Hollywood, and her leftist politics. By midsummer of 1950, they had finished a rough cut of the picture; and their hopes ballooned when delegates from the major studios descended on them and even watched some of the final shooting in anticipation of bidding for distribution in the United States.

Wright went home to Paris without screening or approving the final release print, an unheard of dereliction, even in supposedly unprincipled Hollywood. The picture was previewed on a Pan American stratoclipper on the run between Buenos Aires and Nice, and again in the spring of 1951 in Argentina. Wright was happy with the reviews and itched to see the film that had been placed in the hands of Classic Pictures, a small New York distributor.

Then Wright's hopes caved in, but his own failure to choose the shots and otherwise supervise the final cut is probably the principal cause. The cutters had patched together the best film they could muster. But in the sudden rush of disappointment, after months of misplaced faith, Wright blamed Walter Gould of Classic for what seemed like drastic cuts in the release-print, among them Bigger's killing a rat, shots of a zip gun, plans for a robbery, racial epithets, and dialogue in the trial sequence. All of them are, however, melodramatically present in the surviving print. In Paris he was enraged at the presumed cuts and thought that Gould had become scared by the inquisitorial influence of Senator Joseph McCarthy, who had begun his assault on the left wing of American politics. In France, on the other hand, Chenal feared the Communists would hurt his career if the cut version were screened in France and urged the Red-dominated unions to campaign against distribution of the picture. Wright's only response was to press Chenal to drop his action and at the same time to sooth the Communists by not promoting the film. Meaninglessly, and perhaps *because* of the differing versions, European critics praised the picture and Americans damned it. If Wright had been present at the final printing he would at least have understood where failure lay. Perhaps he did not want the hurt of knowing who really was to blame.

Even if Wright had been correct in his strong feeling that cutting had ruined the picture, nothing could erase the presence of the impossible conditions that attended the film from its beginnings. The multilingual company and remote location closed off even a dribble of the secular wisdom that Hollywood technicians could have offered. They as least would have fought Wright's misbegotten urge to star. There were empty studios on both coasts with dependable crews happy to make a few dollars below union scale. Oscar Micheaux used to shoot in the old Selig studio in Chicago; Dudley Murphy shot *Emperor Jones* in Paramount's Astoria studio; and there were others in the Bronx and on the fringes of Hollywood. Even before shooting Wright watched his novel go through the hands of a famous white playright, a French Communist director, and the distorted prism of several cultures. Even the actors were part of the linguistic and cultural tangle. The best of the cast included only a striking blonde starlet, an American character actor, a charming amateur who played Bessie Mears, and Willa

Pearl Curtis as Bigger's mother. The international cast must have added to the problems by necessitating the eventual dubbing of English over the Latin actors who filled out the *dramatis personae.* The company had to call on their cutters to match the Chicago exteriors with the Argentine studio shots, and then to tighten the rest into a flowing narrative. And there was middle-aged Wright in the midst of everything trying to be Bigger. "It was the damnedest thing you've ever seen," recalled Horace Cayton, one of his oldest Chicago friends.

Exhibitors and bookers knew a "turkey" when they saw one and needed no political or racial reasons for refusing it. Outside of New York few people, even in ghetto movie houses, had an opportunity to see the picture. And Wright realized only a few thousand dollars for three years' work. Moreover, the modest opening was in the middle of summer, the worst of times for any movie, much less one with such a checkered provenance. The newspaper advertising must have shaken Wright even more than the cutting. The lurid mats featured Wright carrying Jean Wallace into the cellar under a stark white headline that blared "The Dynamite Loaded Story of a Negro and a White Girl!" Off in a corner and easily cropped appeared the sole reference to "the most discussed novel of our time . . . the play that rocked Broadway."

One question remains. Was Wright justified in his pique with the cutters? The surviving print reveals that most of those shots Wright believed had been removed in fact remained, and that they contributed more a melodramatic tang than a social indictment of American life. The experience that Wright agonized through may be akin to that of the producer who lounges at his pool in Beverly Hills while the second unit company is out in the desert shooting. No one screens the "dailies"—the cans of exposed film that constitute each day's work. Telephone reports disguise what the producer could see if he went on location and screened the dailies in the local Bijou. Very likely Wright did not see the work in progress and thereby deluded himself with cottony optimism. Moreover, he failed to see the picture through its rough cuts, its answer print, and its final fine grain positive. With Wright gone the

Argentine technicians lacked the artistic supervision essential to turn out a polished product.

All the black proletarian imagery of the novel that seemed to emerge out of Wright's own experience seemed trite and melodramatic in the film. All that remains is the plotty narrative. The "establishing shots"—those that tell the audience where they are—open on, not the ghetto, but a dull view of Michigan Boulevard, with a narrator who sounds like a parody of the dull travelogues of James A. Fitzpatrick. He reads Sandburgian word-pictures while the shots lead into the "black belt," the "prison without bars" where one at a time in stilted order the black characters are introduced: Hannah, Vera, Buddy, Bigger, and even the dead father, killed by lynchers. It is here that Wright introduces the rat he missed in the European print. But the effect is far more comic than socially critical. Bigger goes through the dreams of becoming an explorer or a pilot, eventually settling for a job as chauffeur to rich Mr. Dalton. Set against his ambition is a black bourgeois nightmare of ghetto life, dirty, and dominated by hustlers and night people. Bigger goes to see Bessie as she tries for a job in Ernie's saloon, violently threatens Ernie and warns him off Bessie, then goes off with a zip gun with the corner gang to plan an armed robbery. Unconsciously symbolic of Wright's isolation from the ghetto game, the gang is set off from Bigger by their cool hats in contrast to his tight, square cap. Thrown out of Ernie's, they drift into the grind house where they witness a movie in which a maid is rebuked for feeding the family dog on the ground rather than at the table. Again Wright believed the shots to be missing, probably his agonized reaction to their failure to make the point his words had made in the novel.

With this last exaggerated stereotype of the insensitive rich in his head, a "cut" takes Bigger to the street where he searches for the Daltons, is introduced through the back door as "the Thomas boy," and responds with a dutiful "yessum." Mrs. Dalton, the least villainous of the whites, is conveniently blind, which explains why "she has a deep interest in colored people."

Once Bigger becomes the chauffeur, he cruises the big car

to a striking black belt exterior scene which effectively captures the squalor of the ghetto. Black kids crowd around the car and even Bessie is impressed with "your boss's car." They ride along the lake and Bigger is still within society, counting himself fortunate to have a job. "Sometimes you're up; sometimes you're down," he says, as he and Bessie ride the roller coaster. And you never know, she tells him protectively, warning that he cannot change the world. The shot cuts to blonde Mary Dalton preening while Bigger humbly lights her cigarette, his hand steadied by hers.

Mary Dalton's liberalism spills out shrilly. She advises him to join a union, sits in the front seat, and confesses "After all, I'm on your side." Her white leftist friend is more than militant, she says:

> He has all the answers to your problems. . . .
> He's not like mother and dad doing missionary
> work. He *fights* for the colored people.

Jan, her friend, acts out his radicalism by requiring Bigger to shake hands and by declining to be called Sir. The three go to Ernie's to a prize fight where Mary Dalton portrays every stock Hollywood erotic cliché. Breasts resting pointedly on the bar, she breathes: "What atmosphere! It's electric! I love it!" Bessie intrudes added tension by singing a commercial torch song, "The Dreamin' Kind," that is designed to pass as blues. Mary again spills over: "Isn't she amazing? All colored people are so gifted!" She and Bessie avoid conflict over Bigger when Mary goes to Bessie's dressing room and offers her an orchid as a clear sign that she rejects Bigger: she is the perfect white foil, offering worshipful appreciation and no resistance. Gradually she becomes drunk and Bigger takes her home where he accidentally smothers her while trying to muffle her drunken titters under a pillow. Only her blind mother intrudes, and sees no Bigger.

Later Bigger is clearly an outcast. At work he is nervous as he conceals the killing; at Ernie's the gang hazes him for his "faithful service;" at home his mother nags at him to avoid trouble so as not to mar Buddy's admiration. He turns to Bessie to help him cover and to profit from the accident by trumping up a fake kidnapping-ransom attempt. The audience can see his alienation as he hides in a ruined abandoned house. He dreams now not of the future but only of flight to Harlem, to Canada, anywhere. Newsmen and police sniff closer as he falsely places Mary's boyfriend in an incriminating light. Bigger flees as the circle tightens. Relief from the melodrama comes with another fine shot of the alley through which Bigger must run. The police break into his mother's place and the chase is on. At the derelict house Bessie goes out and hears of a reward for Bigger's capture, and carelessly tips off a street hustler who brings the police. The exterior shots begin to throb with littered streets, careening cops, bursting doors, keening black women, blacks aroused by night raiders. Bigger and the police skitter over the rooftops, stark against the lights. The symbolism grows obvious. Bigger goes up a watertower; rids himself of his white shirt for safety; rejects the mythic baptism and rebirth motif of western literature by scuttling away from the water hosed onto the tank; and finally after shooting a cop edges across a catwalk on a funeral parlor sign. The "intercuts" are to raging mobs in the streets.

At last Bigger is caught. The trial sequence in the novel in which the worst forms of economic oppression are revealed, is all but missing in the film, even the unconscious exploitation by the Daltons, who felt their exhorbitant rents were merely a matter of the impersonality of the law of supply and demand. The film reflects only a lame wish that what has happened will not happen to other blacks. Essentially all that has gone before has no social meaning. All that remains is a poorly wrought melodrama ending in a rooftop chase.

Throughout, Wright revealed himself to be a resourceful and game actor who ultimately failed for want of experience, polish, and consistency. It is difficult, anyway, to act in movies with a steady eye toward character motivation and development. Shots are made in their most economical order, not in narrative sequence. A shot in which a single line is delivered may take all morning to set up and its reaction may take the rest of the afternoon. Most Hollywood moviemakers count it a good day's work if they can manage to finish three or four pages of the shooting script. Because of the widespread location shooting and multilingual production company, remote from the culture in which Wright had produced his book, Wright did as well as possible enacting Bigger. Nevertheless, his accent seemed overly cultured compared with the hip tones of others in the cast, and his stiff movements failed to reflect the cool style of the ghetto. It is clear by the end of the film that Wright had reached the limit of his powers.

Wright's admirers in black and white press circles were appalled. Reacting to what was probably *Native Son*'s only showing on the West Coast, the black *California Eagle* decided it was terrible. The liberal Catholic weekly, *Commonweal*, along with the *New York Times*, felt keen disappointment not only at the stuff of the novel, which was "hard to take when actually visualized," but the production's values as well, which seemed "awkwardly amateurish." New York's black *Amsterdam News* reviewer announced: "I think it stinks." Its only redeeming virtue was Gloria Madison, the young black girl, who played Bessie. Totally inexperienced, the Hunter College graduate seemed to be a surer bet for future success than anyone else in the film.

The worst news of all for Wright came from Hollywood. The pressure brought by Walter White, the general liberal air of the war years, the increasing white awareness of the black ghetto, the slow rise of black stars such as Sidney Poitier and Harry Belafonte, who had dramatic training rather than vaudeville experience, served to stimulate the major studios to dabble in racial problem films such as *Intruder in the Dust, Pinky, No Way Out, Lost Boundaries, The Well* and many others. The all-black cinema of the old "race movies" slowly died in the postwar era. So too did the other extreme of black accomodation to segregation: the Stepin Fetchits of Hollywood. Wright was a victim as well. With Hollywood producing strong statements on race with better facilities, more accomplished technicians, trained actors, the Negro press embraced their productions, and ignored Wright's.

The narrow, unreal world of moviemaking was remote from

the life Wright had written about. And moreover, the demands of shooting in Chicago and Argentina, editing and dubbing in New York, and selling the picture through a small distributor doomed his effort to only the most esoteric cinema circles. The picture, rather than broadening Wright's audience, shrank it into a tight little group of New York aesthetes who could offer him nothing, not even good box office grosses. Like Paul Robeson and Oscar Micheaux before him and the Poitiers and Gordon Parkses and Melvin Van Peebleses after him, he had learned the hard lesson that the most impervious white institution was like Mary Dalton, well meaning, solicitous of black plight, but ultimately useless for the kind of strong black expression that was possible in the solitary medium of fiction.

Richard Wright in Chicago, 1928

"A FRANK, BRUTAL MOVIE! ...WORTH SEEING!"
—Bill Leonard, CBS
"Native Son"
starring
JEAN WALLACE · RICHARD WRIGHT
NICHOLAS JOY
AT LAST ON THE SCREEN!
Torn from the pages of the most discussed novel of our time...the play that rocked Broadway!

Richard Wright's NATIVE SON starring JEAN WALLACE, RICHARD WRIGHT, NICHOLAS JOY and introducing GLORIA MADISON. A Walter Gould Presentation.

Richard Wright's NATIVE SON starring JEAN WALLACE, RICHARD WRIGHT, NICHOLAS JOY and introducing GLORIA MADISON. A Walter Gould Presentation.

Richard Wright's NATIVE SON starring JEAN WALLACE, RICHARD WRIGHT, NICHOLAS JOY and introducing GLORIA MADISON. A Walter Gould Presentation.

Richard Wright at Wading River, L. I., 1947

Let my people go

Richard Wright

HAIKU

by Richard Wright

The crow flew so fast
That he left his lonely caw
Behind in the fields

Just enough of rain
To bring the smell of silk
From the umbrellas

Coming from the woods
A bull has a sprig of lilac
Dangling from a horn

Why is the hail so wild
Bouncing so frighteningly
Only to lie so still

A balmy spring wind
Reminding me of something
I cannot recall

Haiku

The dog's violent sneeze
Fails to rouse a single fly
On his mangy back

I would like a bell
Tolling this soft twilight
Over willow trees

The green cocklebures
Caught in the thick wooly hair
Of the black boy's head

Winter rain at night
Sweetening the taste of bread
And spicing the soup

An empty sickbed
An indented white pillow
In weak winter sun

Exile

Wright's Exile

MICHEL FABRE

Since Richard Wright's death, much has been written about his self-exiled life in Paris and his relationship to America, white or black. During his life, he was frequently attacked in the columns of the American establishment press, and very little was written which aimed to defend him or to explain the near-necessity and the true meaning of his exile. Any attempt to summarize the reactions of the American press to Wright's books from 1946 to the present, or to trace the effect of Wright's supposed "anti-americanism" or American critical attitudes, would amount to a full study in itself. Therefore, I shall only briefly allude to it. Similarly, the attitude of the white American colony and the government services in Paris toward Wright deserves a long analysis of its own. My lecture is thus bound to be somewhat sketchy, and many of the subtleties and intricacies of political attitudes, personal antagonisms, and literary jealousies can only be hinted at. In order to present what I consider the most important facet of Wright's relationship with America while in exile, I shall limit myself to examining Wright's own point-of-view. This point-of-view, deeply logical though sometimes changing, informed his public declarations, his political stands, and even his writing during the late forties and the fifties. This period was of course one of the most tense in American history, witnessing not only the birth of the Cold War but also the frantic rise of McCarthyism—a period during which the pre-war investigations of the Dies Committee seemed innocuous in comparison with the probings of the Senate Sub-committee on Un-American Activities, a period during which Wright certainly would have suffered, had he remained in America, both from his former membership in the Communist Party, and from his vigorous fight against racism. The younger people among you should bear in mind that, a few decades ago, the spoken criticism of one's country was considered dangerous enough to be regarded as sufficient reason for silencing someone—dangerous enough for a writer of the stature of Richard Wright to represent a threat to the image that America was then bent upon disseminating abroad. Hence the historical importance of Wright's own attitude and pronouncements as a critic of America.

* * *

It goes without saying that Richard Wright had been deeply dissatisfied with the black man's place in the American system for a long time, even a long time before he joined the Communist Party (perhaps more as a way of getting out of the cultural ghetto than out of a sense of outrage). It is impossible to find in the whole of his works a single sentence of unreserved praise for his mother country. Nor does one ever encounter in his journal or private correspondence the spontaneous ejaculations of wonder or ease that abound when he thinks about France, though this praise of France is usually quickly followed by criticism. The only glorification of America in his works that I can recall is in a 1936 poem entitled "Transcontinental," but this is a glorification of what America *could be* under a soviet regime. And his review, written in 1945, of the *Complete Works* of Horatio Alger, which he had read so avidly in his youth, shows how completely he had eschewed the myth of the American dream.

His removal to France did not appreciably change his attitude towards the United States, and his exile was more the result of the attitude of white Americans towards him and his image of America than it was the result of his discovering in France a more humane style of life and a freer cultural atmosphere. When he wrote "I Choose Exile" (which *Ebony Magazine* had requested in 1950, but refused to print and which other American magazines prudently discarded), Wright was already trying to explain, if not justify, his choice which was already described as un-American in 1951. He was on the defensive, thus, he was picking his words cautiously, and weighing them, when he wrote:

> I'll define my idea of freedom, though I'm certain I run the risk of being branded as Un-American. If I am, then I readily plead guilty; but I insist I am *not* Anti-American, which, to me, is the important thing.
>
> My Un-Americanism, then, consists of the fact that I want the right to hold, without fear of punitive measures, an opinion with which my neighbor does not agree; the right to travel wherever and whenever I please even though my ideas might not coincide with those of whatever Federal Administration might be in power in Washington; the right to express publicly my distrust of the "collective wisdom" of the people; the right to exercise my conscience and intelligence to the extent of refusing to "inform" and "spy" on my neighbor because he holds political convictions differing from mine; the right to express, without fear of reprisal, my rejection of religion.
>
> These Un-American sentiments add up to a fundamental right which I insist upon, the right to live free of mob violence, whether that violence assumes the guise of an anonymous blacklisting or of pressure exerted through character assassination ("I Choose Exile," unpublished ms., pp. 1-2).

At that time, Wright was forced to define his attitude toward America in relationship to what was taking place in the US, where the tensions due to the Cold War had turned the administration into a kind of super-surveillance bureau. A few years earlier, his attitude had been very different: he did not take a political stand in favor of individual rights and democracy so much as he criticized American mass culture. In a 1946 letter to Gertrude Stein, he alluded to Phillip Wylie's *Generation of Vipers* and Henry Miller's *The Air-Conditioned Nightmare,* preferring Wylie's book as the stronger of the two, because, in his opinion, Wylie fought America as an American, and Miller fought America as an American who went to Europe. He concluded:

> I'm very interested in this matter how one regards one's country. It is very easy to damn America by rejecting America and it is very hard to damn America while accepting

> America. Most of the new generation of writers have no illusions about America, yet they feel themselves above all as Americans. I criticize America as an American and you do too, which I think is the only real way to do the job. Miller's rejection of America seems to me the act of a weak man (Wright to Gertrude Stein, April 12, 1946).

This distinction between criticizing America as an American and rejecting America as an expatriate is an important one because, to the end of his life in exile, Wright did not yield to the temptation, which would have been amply justified by the reactions of official America to him, to reject America. He hoped America could be transformed and that his criticism could be of help in the process. Such is clearly his attitude in 1952, when he has had plenty of opportunities to see his country from afar and to gauge foreign reactions to it. "I Choose Exile" ends with these words:

> Yet, exile though I am, I remain unalterably and simply American and, as such, I've often asked myself, if, armed with these gloomy insights garnered from an exiled life, I could somehow aid my country in its clumsy grappling with alien realities; if I could somehow warn Americans against a too self-righteous display of wealth in the face of a naked and shivering world; if I could in some way inject into the American consciousness a consciousness of *their* consciousness. . . . Daily press dispatches and tourist word of mouth descriptions of what is transpiring back home make me doubtful. Would not such advice sound suspiciously like Communist propaganda? Would it not seem to place a morally objectionable question mark after our fondest convictions of the invulnerability of material might? Any offer of help of that sort might well merit a militant attack on the part of those determined, in their shortsightedness, to defend at any cost their American purity. . . . So I watch my country from afar, but with no sense of glee, no smug self-satisfaction; rather it is with a strange perturbation of heart ("I Choose Exile," pp. 16-17).

As the years passed, and the hostility against him grew, however, Wright's attitude began to change. Let us now examine the forms this hostility took, and how it affected the writer in exile.

One of the first incidents Wright had encountered apropos of his going to France had been, after the "friendly" advice offered by several New York acquaintances to dissuade him from going, a disguised refusal of the State Department to grant him a passport. Finally, thanks to the intervention of Gertrude Stein's friends, like Chagall's son-in-law, French cultural attaché Claude Levi-Strauss offered Wright an official invitation, making it impossible for the government to withhold a passport without an official explanation to the French diplomats. Thus, the State Department completely reversed its attitude: officially, Wright was to be in charge of some American paintings loaned to the French government for an exhibition. After having been prohibited from going, he was reluctantly made a kind of ambassador in the hope that he would moderate his remarks on American race relations. The American Embassy in Paris tried to woo Wright at first. He relates the following anecdote in "I Choose Exile": "At a cocktail party a strange white American took me discretely aside and whispered in my ear: 'Listen, for God's sake, don't let these foreigners make you into a brick to hurl at our windows!' I realized that a bare recital, when uttered in an alien atmosphere, of the facts of Negro life in America constituted a kind of anti-American propaganda." (p. 8).

Wright always refused to play the game. He answered the questions of the French journalists frankly, he told it "like it was," and naturally the gap between him and the people at the American Embassy quickly widened.

I would like to digress here a moment to distinguish between the reactions of the Embassy people to Wright's presence and his statements, and the attitude of white Americans in Paris toward him. Because of his race, Wright was kept at a distance by most WASP members of the American colony. Of course, he never tried to win their acceptance, since he hated their company and the kind of shallow social life they were leading. Apart from a few personal friends and acquaintances among the American whites, Wright received a friendly welcome from the Reverend Clayton Williams, at that time pastor of the American Church in Paris, the directors and staff of the

American Library in Paris, especially Harry Goldberg, several other government employees at the American Cultural Center, and most of the staff of the American Center for Students and Artists and the Benjamin Franklin library. On the whole, there was far less racial prejudice among government officials and employees than among the rich WASP set, American firms in general, and even the American Hospital in Neuilly. But, because the employees of the Embassy represented the policy of the government, Wright encountered among them an understandably larger opposition on political grounds, especially when Senator McCarthy sent Roy Cohn on a European trip to put pressure on US libraries to ban so-called un-American books.

At that time, Wright was notorious for opposing the Marshall plan, for siding with the coalition of left-wing groups called Rassemblement Démocratique Révolutionnaire both against the United States and the Soviet Union, and for his interviews in French newspapers denouncing racism on American soil. He then even went further: he tried to fight racism in the American colony in Paris itself. This was, along with his hope of creating a rapprochement between progressive and liberal French intellectuals and their American counterparts, one of the major aims of the short-lived but by no means negligible French-American Fellowship Association which he founded in 1949. I personally think that James Baldwin is unfair to the association in his "Alas, Poor Richard" article. He describes it as "one of the most improbable and old-fashioned of English melodramas" *(NKN,* Delta edition, p. 208) and pretends not to have taken it seriously, but the record shows that he took it seriously enough at the time to attend more than one meeting and to assume the responsibility of investigating the employment opportunities for black Americans and the racist policy of white US firms in Paris. After a flagrant instance of racial discrimination in the hiring of a nurse at the American hospital, The Franco-American Fellowship held a press conference, and Wright gave a long interview to *France Observateur* (later published in *Crisis,* June 1950, under the title "American Negroes in France."). The incident was greatly publicized by the French press, and, although Wright received several indignant letters from white Americans, none of them could disprove his statements. During the first half of 1950, Wright and other members of the association were busy asking the Supreme Court to intervene in the case of the seven black boys at Martinsville, who had been found guilty of rape and sentenced. Above all, they helped M.R.A.P., the major French organization against racism to build up a wide campaign in favor of Willie McGee, and later raised funds for his widow and children.

Wright never lost a chance to denounce American racism in all its aspects. Thanks to him, the image of the United States that the French public held was a little removed from the image broadcast by official propaganda. Hence the inimical reactions from the Embassy. During the period in which McCarthyism was most virulent, the situation became critical for Wright: had he been expelled from France under any pretext, he would have had to face the Committee on Un-American Activities at home. Besides, it was not uncommon for American citizens abroad trying to renew their passports to have them confiscated when these citizens were too openly critical of their government. Wright lived in constant fear of this and thus he had to reinforce his friendships with the few people he knew in the French government, even at the cost of maintaining a public silence about the Algerian war in the following years. An instance of this concern can be found in a letter he wrote to the editor of the *Yale Law Journal* on May 5, 1952, in response to its article "Passport Refusals for Political Reasons":

> As an American living abroad . . . what struck me was that the article dealt with so few cases of the State Department's refusing to grant passports . . . Would the writer be interested in gaining contact with other people who had their passports taken from them? If so, I can put him in touch with at least three others.
>
> The purpose of this letter is to beg a world of information from the writer. If the State Department notifies an American citizen living abroad that his passport has been cancelled, and if the passport remains in possession of the

> owner and is not stamped cancelled, and if the American citizen refuses to surrender said passport, what law is he violating? The passport in question, let us suppose, has just been renewed for a period of two years. . . . In asking this question I'm assuming of course that the American citizen in question is not attempting to avoid legal sanctions, that he is living in a country where the United States government does not have to protect him.

It is clear that Wright had no theoretical case in mind; rather, he was preoccupied with his own status and what he would have to do, were his passport actually cancelled.

But Wright was allowed to remain in Paris. America dealt with him in other ways, sometimes far more subtly. During the fifties, and especially after the publication of *The Outsider,* the reaction of American critics and the American press in general toward Wright's books was one of dissatisfaction at his remaining away or at his being critical of American policy in the Third World. A more or less disguised attempt was made to dismiss Wright's criticism of America as politically and culturally irrelevant, under the pretense that he had been away too long or that he had been blinded by Communism (although he had repudiated it) and by existentialism. Most of the adverse criticism boiled down to the unformulated accusation of "unamericanness," of dealing in foreign ideologies, or alien philosophies, of having forsaken the good old American truths. I must stress, however, that there was comparatively little criticism of that sort in the form of reviews of the books Wright published while in exile. We must not imagine that there was a vast conspiracy of silence towards him and that it worked; rather McCarthyism and the changing times had apparently made the American audience unmindful of what Wright had to say. Some critics still maintain that, indeed, Wright's work had then become irrelevant to the American scene, but let me avoid that point of controversy for now.

The most striking instances of unfavorable criticism of Wright's attitudes are, in my opinion, to be found in an invidious article written for *The Reporter* by Negro journalist Ben Burns in 1956, and in the slanderous way *Time* magazine reproached Wright with "Living Amid the Alien Corn" in 1957.

Ben Burns, whom Wright knew personally, had been one of the *Ebony Magazine* editors who had refused "I Choose Exile" in 1952. At the time, Wright had courteously replied: "Frankly I have come to feel . . . that the sentiments I expressed in that article were a little too strong for your magazine. I don't quarrel with you for this. You are on the home scene and you know better than I do what kind of an impression you want *Ebony* to make" (Wright to the Editors of *Ebony Magazine,* January 23, 1953). After a while, Wright had finally managed to have his piece returned in order to send it to the *Atlantic Monthly.* When that magazine also refused it, he declared to Reynolds: "It simply means that fear has reached even to Boston. Being far away from America gives me a kind of insight into the country which, perhaps, even those there do not have. It just means that one can't praise even the culture of an ally, and France is our official ally" (Wright to Reynolds, January 30, 1953). He even went so far as to promise Reynolds that he would only talk about the effects of industrialization, and in a non-committed, "non-national" way, to the *New York Times* reporters who were supposed to interview him. He was therefore surprised and angered when he read Burns' attack in *The Reporter.* Among criticism in general of the Black circle in Paris, which he called "Café society," Burns wrote that:

> Wright's venom, retailed constantly by expatriates at sidewalk cafés plus years of headlines about Dixie lynching has succeeded in poisoning European thinking about racial problems in America. No amount of documents on the change of status of the US Negro, no statistics . . . avail to revise these European opinions. Richard Wright enjoys a good audience on the Left Bank for his hate school of literature ("They're Not Uncle Tom's Children," *The Reporter*, March 8, 1956, p. 22.).

Burns went on to prove, quite rightly, that there was racism in France, that Wright did not dare talk about the Algerian war for fear of being expelled, that the average American Negro was better off financially than many Frenchmen. But in shamelessly resorting to these arguments, he was only repeating the old tricks used by any country to turn away criticism of its racial policies. Wright's reactions to the matter are contained in a letter to Reynolds: "It is simply foolish to say that I poisoned the mind of Europe; if that is true, I am more powerful than either Moscow or Peking. . . . Ben Burns saw me only in one café where he asked to be taken. . . . To my mind, subversion is a legal business and I felt that Burns was taking the role of the Attorney General when he said that I bordered on the subversive," he wrote on April 13, 1956. Afterward, Wright staunchly refused to have anything to do with "that individual."

The other important episode consisted in *Time Magazine* attributing to Wright a sentence he had never spoken in an interview he had never granted. In a Nov. 17, 1958 article entitled "Amid the Alien Corn," attacking Black expatriates in Paris, Wright was said to have declared, among other things, that "The Negro problem in America has not changed in three hundred years." Now, on another occasion Wright could have said that the mind and mood of white America had not changed much in three centuries, but such a phrasing of his thought was inaccurate, and besides, he had not said that to a *Time* reporter, since he had refused to grant an interview. *Time* had used Gisele Freund to photograph him, and then afterward, concocted a false interview.

Wright tried to fight *Time.* Gisele Freund wrote a declaration for him, dated Nov. 22, 1958, in which she said: "Contrary to the report and the impression created by *Time* magazine, I state emphatically that I did not interview you for *Time* magazine," and she noted that at the time she did not know who had commissioned the photographs. On Nov. 25, 1958, *Time* magazine wrote to Wright's lawyers in New York: "The photographer immediately reported the quotations to *Time*'s Paris Bureau. . . . Moreover the quotations seem to be Mr. Wright's sentiment concerning this country. . . . Furthermore I do not believe that the quotations attributed to Mr. Wright are in any way actionable according to our libel laws or the laws of France. In the circumstances, the editors of *Time* will not consider publishing any retraction settling your client's claim."

Wright did not sue, since he could not have gotten more than the symbolic dollar for damages, but he achieved a kind of victory, nevertheless. The Paris bureau of the magazine refrained in the future from attacking other expatriates: "They claimed," Wright wrote Paul Reynolds, "that they were inspired by another article appearing in a British periodical . . . planted by an American to start an international fuss about American Negroes living in France (Wright to Reynolds, Nov. 19, 1958), adding in another letter, "The local *Time* let it leak out that they had gathered a whole batch of letters hostile to me from their *Time* readers and they were going to run them. I think we stopped that" (Wright to Reynolds, Dec. 8, 1958).

I shall not go into details, but this attack and the tactics used by *Time* magazine certainly were part of a wider effort to discredit Black expatriates and to make their expulsion easier if they could not be silenced. These were the typical Cold War methods of dealing with embarrassing people. Wright provided an excellent analysis of such tactics long before radical magazines like *Ramparts* revealed the many connections and fronts of the CIA. He expounded on these tactics in his last lecture, given at the American Church in Paris in early November, 1960. He denounced, for example, the system used by America to control American Negroes in these terms:

> It is a deadly fight in which brother is set against brother, in which threats of physical violence are hurled by one black to another, where vows to cut or kill are voiced.. . . Having lived on the fringes of that system, I feel free to speak of it; I think I've grasped its outlines with a certain degree of objectivity. . . . My speaking of it has this aim: perhaps I can make you aware of the tragic tensions and frustrations which such a system of control inflicts upon Negro artists and intellectuals" ("The Position of the Negro Artist and Intellectual in American Society," unpublished lecture, p. 11).

Wright proceeded to depict the Black American's struggle against economic reality and psychological conditioning. He felt that politically, the Communist stance was often inimical to the Negro, but that the United States government was afraid of his communism. He believed that the statement Paul Robeson had made in 1949, that the Negroes in America would not fight against Russia, was foolish and irresponsible, yet the US government had apparently taken that threat seriously. Robeson had been blacklisted and ousted, perhaps not so much because the government was afraid of him but because he represented alien ideas circulating among Negroes. Communism was merely a pretense, for any other doctrine would have served as well, Wright added. He then analyzed the methods through which ideological control was achieved, through spying, through infiltrating potentially revolutionary organizations with black undercover agents of the FBI or CIA:

> Obviously we are entering a period where complete control over the ideology seeping into the Black belts cannot be completely maintained. Books, mass means of communication, the developing tourist habits of the Negro, have broken down the walls ... Negroes who harbored revolutionary ideas were not talking, they were wary. They had to be found and identified ... Hence Negroes who could talk Communism were sent into the Black Belts. Indeed I'd say that there is more Communism being talked among Negroes today than ever but it is a false Communism; the language of the informer, the spy. . . . I'd go so far as to say that most Communism in the Black Belts today is sponsored by the American government. I'll go further, I'll say that most revolutionary movements in the Western world are government-sponsored; they are launched by agents provocateurs to organize the discontented so that the government can keep an eye on them ("The Position of the Negro Artist and Intellectual in American Society," unpublished lecture, pp. 23-24).

Wright had spotted several black spies operating in Paris, and he said half-jokingly: "Sometimes I have patriotic moods and I have dreamed of setting up in Paris a bureau to invent identities for stray Negro spies" ("The Position of the Negro Artist and Intellectual in American Society," unpublished lecture, p. 24 b). Wright resolutely tried to confront that situation for the sake of fighting political and moral corruption: "I think that mental health urges us to bring all of these hidden things into the open where they can be publicly dealt with. What have I been describing to you? I've been describing various forms of moral corruption—corruption which has its roots in fear and greed " ("The Position of the Negro Artist and Intellectual in American Society," unpublished lecture, p. 34).

Before we continue with Wright's delineation of the governmental methods of control over the black man, I would like to answer a few questions that have undoubtedly crept into your minds: For example, if Wright knew that the CIA sponsored many so-called progressive organizations, why did he himself deal with these organizations, and even accept money from them?

First of all, Wright was unaware at the beginning that the Congress for Cultural Freedom, which had been set up in 1951, I believe, was indirectly controlled by the CIA. He gave several lectures for their Paris bureau, and wrote articles for *Preuves* and *Encounter* magazines. In fact, he went to Bandung on their money, but I must add that he insisted on the conditions that he would not represent anybody other than himself, that he would not accept any kind of censorship and that he would speak freely of whatever he would see. I must also add, in all fairness, that the people in charge agreed to all this and kept their promise. Afterwards, in the late fifties, they wanted Wright to go to India and give lectures there, hoping that this would serve their propaganda, but he refused and things remained at that point, all contact between them ceasing.

When, shortly after the 1956 Congress of Black Writers and Artists, the American Section of the Society of African Culture was founded, Wright knew that several of its members had tacitly agreed to play the game of the US government as regards negritude, Pan-Africanism and African politics. He collaborated with them as long as he thought that what they were doing could, in one way or another, serve the aims of African nationalism and decolonization. But when he found out that help from them came only with strings attached, he refused it. In 1959, he applied for a grant of several thousand dollars in order to go to West Africa again and to do a story on ex-French colonies. John A. Davis, then AMSAC president, apparently feared that what Wright would say might harm the position of AMSAC and, in that case, AMSAC would not want to sponsor Wright's book, thus getting nothing for their money. (John A. Davis to Wright, May 2, 1959). "After due reflection," Wright answered, "I have come to the conclusion that the prospect of doing 'harm' would psychologically cripple me in trying to gather material on French Africa. . . . I'd not like to go there with the feeling that I'd have to inhibit myself in whatever I'd write. I think that the wiser course for me would be to seek more disinterested sponsorship. By doing so I'm personally responsible for what I'd write and the public reaction " (Wright to John A. Davis, June 3, 1959). The tone of this letter is friendly, but it clearly indicates where Wright drew the line in any compromise.

Now let us return to Wright's exposure of the American government's handling of American Negro protest organizations and nationalist movements in Africa and his description of the effect of McCarthyism on Black expatriates in Paris. It should be kept in mind that these remarks of his were prompted more by a desire to open people's eyes than by a desire to strike back at the personal attacks he himself had undergone. During his last lecture, Wright repeatedly used personal examples and mentioned names of Black writers who had been involved in such disputes, but only to make his disclosures believable. He was much more interested in dealing with general policies and principles. Speaking of Black writers, he said at the beginning of his talk:

> Their words can be disputed, and this disputation does not apply to figures or facts but to attitudes. For example, the white writers and critics of America find it morally correct to hurl criticisms at a Negro writer if he lectures about the race problem, say, in Sweden. He is told that it is better to "wash dirty clothes at home" rather than in public or where Communists can hear him. There are times when the white American press, periodicals such as *Time* or *Life* will castigate a Negro novelist not for what he says but for the geographical position which he has taken up on earth. Hence a Negro American writer living in Paris will be sneered at

> in the white press of America for having chosen to live there. Naturally a white writer does not come in for such critical blastings ("The Position of the Negro Artist and Intellectual," unpublished lecture, p. 1).

Wright was clearly trying to vindicate the Black American writer's right to speak out, for himself, for the Black Community, for the world. He felt the duty of the Afro-American writer lay in defending not only the rights of the Negro but the rights of man; and he could do so in a more efficient and more objective way when criticizing his own country from a distance:

> At home I had spent half of my life advocating the rights of the Negro and I knew that if my fight was not right, then nothing was right. Yet I always felt a sneaking sense of futility because I knew there was something basically wrong in a nation that could so cynically violate its own Constitution and democratic pretensions by meting out physical and psychological cruelties to a defenseless minority. From the distance of a freer culture, my feelings somewhat changed. Anger turned into a sort of amazed pity, for I felt that America's barbaric treatment of the Negro was not one-half so bad as the destructive war which she waged, in striking at the Negro, against the Rights of Man, and against herself! ("The Position of the Negro Artist and Intellectual," p. 11).

It was clearly not a question of personal reactions, whether to racism or to the pressures of the State Department, so much as a matter of principles, of acting in the way Wright believed a true American should act. For we must not be mistaken. In spite of a strong temptation to resign his citizenship near the very end of his life, Wright never ceased to be a loyal American citizen, loyal to his country, not as it was at the time but as he imagined it could be one day: a country whose nationality would be defined through all the components and races which form it, and not purely through the dominant groups or classes which claimed to represent 100% America. Seen in these terms, the question of Wright's Americanness or un-Americanness becomes nearly irrelevant.

This question of Wright's Americanness was nowhere better defined than in a piece he wrote, probably in the late fifties, for delivery to a French audience. To the question "Am I an American?" Wright gave not one, but some eighty-six answers, each one beginning with "I am an American, but . . ." and the "but," of course, is the important point. (The order of the eighty-six answers in the unfinished and often illegible draft is arbitrary and Wright would probably have reorganized the sequence; I have therefore taken the liberty of grouping related answers in order to stress the main lines of his thinking. In the following quotation from this piece, the numbers appearing at the end of the quotation are those of each answer.)

Briefly, Wright appears to be proud of his country's past and some of its present achievements, but not at the expense of any other nation; he does not feel that the US is the end-product of all history, holding the only truth. He is ashamed of her racial and imperialistic policies at home and abroad, her religious and political intolerance, her way of buying off leaders of the Third World, of labelling Africa as primitive and despicable. He regrets that the United States was not first in declaring war on Nazi Germany and that it supported the fascist regimes of Franco, Batista, and Syngman Rhee. He feels that the so-called melting pot has never melted anything and that the WASPs are still apeing the cultural standards of Europe to the detriment of indigenous creation.

In opposition to what he has always deplored in American civilization—even by 1942 he was describing Americans as "lovers of trash"—Wright gradually forms a definition of what he means by American, in a style strongly reminiscent of Gertrude Stein's roundabout way of staying with a theme or an idea. We can find in it a vindication of Wright's exile:

> I am an American but tomorrow I could surrender my citizenship and still be an American (49).
>
> I am an American but I can live without America and still be an American, which ought to—I feel—prove what an American is or ought to be (64).
>
> I am an American but I would rather surrender being an American so that the American in me can be believed (66).

> I am an American but I feel most American when I no longer know that I am an American, for I feel that being an American ought to mean freedom from the psychological cruelty of being solely identified as one (36).
>
> I am an American but I insist upon talking about the meaning of being an American because I know that being an American means more to the world and mankind than what is defined in being an American today (58).
>
> I am an American but I am persuaded that America means infinitely more than she thinks she means to the world today (65).

So far we see that Wright insists upon two points: first, Today's America contrasted with what it was yesterday, and second, that America is more than she thinks she is, opposing therefore, the international idea to the national one.

Rather surprisingly, Wright also insists on the value of tradition: "I am an American, but I realize and sense the meaning of my revolt that made me an American can be sensed and felt at its deepest only in relation to that rich and fecund Europe against which America once rebelled" (17). Elsewhere he alludes to 1776 and to Emerson's self-reliance as a universal concept. And he adds, Whitman-like: "I am an American, but perhaps of the kind you have forgotten, self-reliant, irritated with authority, full of praise for those who can stand alone, respecting the sacredness that I feel resides in the human personality" (46). He extolls individualism and personal responsibility, which sets him apart, in his eyes, from the "flock" of mass society. He appeals to a sense of the past: "I am an American, but not of today's America, tense, frightened, too self-conscious to be confident and humane in its leadership of the world for which it seeks to speak" (5). "I am an American but not afraid of Communism, feeling that the revolution launched by my nation is as powerful (if we Americans would ever believe it!) as any launched anywhere" (47). "I am an American, but chosen migrations, a multiplicity of social adjustments in many lands and many climes have made me feel that I could, as an American, live here among you without feeling that I am among moral inferiors; indeed, I am that sort of

American—an amalgam of many races and many continents and cultures, that I feel that the real end and aim of being an American is to be able to live as a man anywhere" (12).

I am not an American myself but I feel moved by this beautiful definition Wright gave of his nation as something international. Other statements make this intellectual definition the more moving because we realize the suffering he underwent in order to cling to his definition of what an American should be. To his French audience, he could proudly declare:

> I am an American but for the twenty-four years that I have been a professional writer I have never used my pen to extoll American humanity at the expense of other people, nor have I sought to degrade other peoples' mores or national habits to the advantage of my country (2). . . . I would die for my country rather than lie for my country (43).

He was bound to deplore and condemn modern America's too exclusive concern for comfort, wealth, and material values:

> I am an American but I can live without air-conditioning, without hot and cold running water, and without tranquilizers (19).
>
> I am an American but I need not use the ideals of my country as an excuse to ask you to give me access to the minerals or the strategic positions of your country (38).
>
> I am an American but I could not dream of insulting or corrupting the human spirit by offering dollars as inducements for others following my way of life (9).
>
> I am an American but I refuse to take part in the secret moral swindle that would make me feel that because Mr. Khrushchev is a white man, I'd rather deal with him and swallow communism—which I probably claim I hate—and fight a so-called Red China because it is yellow (72).

All of Wright's choices are, again, summed up in the declaration: "I am an American but I dream of being able to live in a world where race, dollars and status are not the final definition of human life" (20). "I think that 'why' is as important as 'how'" (41). This is a philosopher's phrase, demonstrating an ultimate concern for metaphysics or eschatology, a capsule of Wright's thinking about the meaning of human life. He is an individualist and a humanist who fights any restrictive definition of man, even if cast in the form of a great American ideal. In that sense he embodies some of the best qualities America has ever produced, and, no doubt, many of you have probably noticed how modern his attitude is and how relevant to our present concerns with freedom, the cultural revolution, and the making of a world civilization. It is all the more heart-breaking to hear him say:

> I am an American but had I not fled my native land, I would have perished in the atmosphere of political hysteria of McCarthyism and I would not have been able to stand here before you (82).
>
> I am an American but I try to keep my heart from freezing in a cold war I never made (70).

* * *

Most of the texts quoted are unpublished, and are printed here with the gracious permission of Mrs. Ellen Wright.

Letter from Richard Wright

(to Owen Dodson)

June 9, 1946
c/o Gallimard
5 rue Sebastien-Bottin
Paris VII, France

Dear Owen:

My trip to France took place so suddenly that I did not have time to get in touch with any of my friends until the last moment, and only a few of them at that. As you may know, I'm over here for a spell as a cultural guest of the French government. I've been here now a month, and most of my so-called duties are over. I hope to start seeing some of this beautiful city of Paris, which is really a kind of garden. Life is tough here for the French people, with food sky high. Only foreigners seem able to live well. All of which makes me realize that there are no good countries any more; there might be a few good spots, but most of the earth today is the same: hunger for jobs, food, houses . . . It is the same as with the folks down in Mississippi, but here it happens with a tiny bit more of beauty and grace.

One of the reasons that compel me to write you now is my memory of your description of what you saw on your Mississippi trip. What you told me is truly important, and since I've been here in Paris I've been wondering if you really realize just how important. The French people, like ours, are also ignorant of the Negro. The forces of commerce have done a damn good job in painting the Negro as something exotic, as a race of people with something queer in them that makes them write jazz music. I wonder if American Negroes really realize the vast harm that they are doing their cause by making themselves into something unreal, something that always sings, something that is always childish? While the great body of their life experiences are untouched and unexpressed? There is no reason why the Negro point of view cannot be put over in Europe, if the right people come over here. There are thousands of Frenchmen who know of our jazz, and no one here seems to realize the great tragedy of the Negro in America, or the meaning of his life. But few could really understand your poem about the Negro mother praying . . . All of this is by way of saying that I do hope and wish that you continue to dig into the rich materials of Negro life and lift them up for all to see, and you ought to know while doing it that you'll be doing more than holding up Negro life for others to see, but you will be holding up human life in all of its forms for all to see. The more we dig into Negro life, the more we are digging into human life.

My work is already being translated over here, and the astonishment, bewilderment which greets it makes me know that they have never had an opportunity to look straight at Negro life. People just do not know what to say or think. It confounds them. They had been led to look at the Negro and laugh; well, they are learning to look at him and let their mouths fall open. So far, there is no opposition here to looking at the Negro honestly. They've just never had a chance to do so before now. So you must realize that it is your duty to keep plugging.

Say, once while in your office you told me that Ira Reid has amassed a pile of stuff on the Dozens. You said that you'd write and get a ms. and send it to me. I had to leave before I could ask you about this. Can you still do it? I'd like like all hell to show such stuff to Frenchmen who are keenly intelligent and would understand it. Do write Reid and if you get the stuff please ship it to me at the above address.

How is Frank? Is his book going? I hope so. Tell him to slave and sweat away at it, as that is the only way.

I'm sorry that illness prevented our talking during my last weeks in New York, but maybe you might be coming over here before I get back home? Why not work towards seeing this part of the world? It is worth it.

Uncle Tom's Children will be published over here in two volumes. Native Son is in the process of being translated. Black Boy will come out later. 12,000,000 Black Voices is being considered. Native Son the play is slated for winter or spring production in Zurich, London and Paris . . . The French literary weeklies are carrying my stories, and I'm writing articles for some French dailies. Ellen and Julia are well; and Julia spends her days in the Luxembourg Gardens, which is really a garden, boy, with blocks of greenery and fountains.

Keep on remembering what you saw in Mississippi and remember that more than half of the human race lives that way . . . And if you do get hold of any Dirty Dozens, send me some . . .

Best to you. I remain,

Sincerely yours,
s/ Dick

* * *

Letters to Richard Wright

Notes and translations by Michel Fabre

Tuesday

Dear Richard Wright:

I have just read *Black Boy*. It needed to be said, and you said it well. Though I am afraid (I am speaking now from the point of view of one who believes that the man who wrote *Native Son* is potentially an artist) it will accomplish little of what it should accomplish, since only they will be moved and grieved by it who already know and grieve over this situation.

You said it well, as well as it could have been said in this form. Because I think you said it much better in *Native Son*, I hope you will keep on saying it, but I hope you will say it as an artist, as in *Native Son*. I think you will agree that the good lasting stuff comes out of one individual's imagination and sensitivity to and comprehension of the suffering of Everyman, Anyman, not out of the memory of his own grief.

A friend of yours lives in my town, Joe Brown. He has shown me his verse. I have (I hope) helped him to learn what you learned yourself: that to feel and believe is not enough to write from. He has not read enough. He has taken my advice lately. The things he has sent me since I have been here (since June) are improving. I am returning to Oxford, Miss. next week, when I shall see him.

Yours sincerely,
s/William Faulkner

Big Sur, California
11/3/46

Dear Richard Wright—

I wrote my friend Beauford Delaney recently to ask for your address, never dreaming you were in France. I had just finished reading *Black Boy* and wanted to let you know immediately how deeply it impressed me. (I have not read any other of your works.) Above all, I was eager to know if you intended to bring out a sequel to it. I want so much to know what happened after you had begun to write. Your reference to Mencken, to the authors he touched upon (the visit to the library—that whole episode) was most touching to me—perhaps because all those authors you mentioned were so close to me, being the very ones I read just before beginning to write.

Then too I had wanted to urge you to send a copy, for translation, to France and Italy. But no doubt you are already published in many European countries. I hope so. I hope in Russia too, and China.

Should you be seeing Raymond Queneau, chez Gallimard, give him my warm greetings.

And my very best wishes to you and all your people every where.

Sincerely,
s/Henry Miller

Mr. Richard Wright
c/o Gallimard
5 rue S. Bottin
Paris (VII)

Turin, 29th August 1947

Dear Mr. Wright,

we are proud to send you two copies of the Italian translation of your book *Black Boy* which, issued in the Spring, is already in reprint. It was a great success here in Italy, owing to its message of sweat and blood and its cutting and virile style. Surely, you don't need any cheering from Italy, but perhaps you'll be interested to learn that we, who have seen so much, consider you among the greatest and most serious writers of to-day.

We are sorry not to be able to publish your other book, *Native Son,* which was purchased by another firm, but hope, keeping in contact with you, to have the previlege [sic] to see first your next book and translate it.

We are yours sincerely

s/Cesare Pavese
Giulio Einaudi Editore

April 25, 1946

Mr. Richard Wright
82 Washington Place
New York, New York

Dear Mr. Wright:

It gives me great pleasure to inform you that the French Government extends to you a cordial invitation to visit France as an official guest and that we shall be glad to take care of your travelling expenses and a month's stay in France.

I understand however that you have already taken care of your ship reservation and that you plan to leave very shortly. In order not to delay you, I would recommend that you do not change your plans and that you ask the "Direction Générale des Relations Culturelles" in Paris (78 rue de Lille), upon your arrival, to refund your expenses, as offered by a cable No. 362 of April 17th from that office.

I shall be at your disposal to complete these informations and to communicate with our Paris office to make the necessary arrangements.

Please believe me,

Very sincerely yours
s/Claude Lévi-Strauss

Sorry not to be able to assist at your merry meeting. I should have been glad to welcome and to congratulate our "confrère" Wright and, through him, all his black brothers. I feel for them since my youth a peculiar and particular sympathy. The first time it was possible for me to realize an important travel, I was propelled by my proneness and my humour towards Central Africa, where I lived almost a year the most happy and interesting days of my life, in direct and continual contact with the true, genuine, decent and naked black people. Finding again afterwards white specimens of humanity, they seemed to me in the first days as under-cooked individuals (des gens mal-cuits). It was a disagreeable, a very painful impression, which happily did not last.

Sitôt de retour en France, j'ai lutté et fait mon possible pour obtenir quelques améliorations dans la situation de ces races depuis si longtemps opprimées. Et ceci m'a valu d'excellentes amitiés, en particulier en Amérique, à l'Université noire d'Atlanta. Longtemps privés de la possibilité de se faire entendre, réduits au mutisme pour ainsi dire, et même n'ayant pas pris conscience (sinon en musique) de ce qu'ils avaient à nous dire ni pu délivrer au monde leur message encore *inoui,* grâces soient rendues à Wright par qui, enfin, ils vont pouvoir se faire entendre.

s/André Gide

Note:

Gide could not write well in English and, as the French commonly do, he used "peculiar" for "special," and "humour" for "disposition." The second half of the note reads:

As soon as I came back to France, I fought and did all I could to obtain some improvements in the situation of those races so long oppressed. And thanks to this I enjoyed excellent friendships, particularly in America, at Atlanta University. For a long time deprived of the possibility of being heard, reduced to muteness, so to speak, and even not being conscious (except in music) of what they had to tell us nor able to deliver their still *unheard* message to the world, let thanks be given to Wright through whom, at last, they are going to be heard.

Paris, 43 rue de Beaune -5, rue Sébastien Bottin (VII°)
16 octobre,

Cher Wright,
Il n'y avait pas de mal vraiment. On a regretté de ne pas vous avoir, voilà tout. A cause de la sympathie, qui est vive. Mais nous trouverons une autre occasion, si vous voulez bien revenir avec Sartre boire le verre de l'amitié. Nous parlerons en même temps des projets de Dorothy Norman.

Cordialement à vous,
s/Albert Camus

Translation:
It was really all right. We only regretted that you could not come, because of our feeling for you, which is strong. But we shall find another opportunity if you agree to come again with Sartre for a drink between friends. At the same time, we shall talk about Dorothy Norman's projects.

Notes:

Wright had been invited to a meeting which he couldn't attend.

The project was that of publishing essays by Sartre, Camus, Simone de Beauvoir and leading French and European intellectuals in a special issue of *Twice A Year*. This enables us to date the letter Oct. 16, 1946 or 1947.

Lundi

Mon cher Wright,
Simone m'apprend que vous êtes provisoirement gèné. Je suis très fâché que vous n'ayiez pas songé à vous adresser à moi. Je vous jure que si j'avais été aus USA dans le même cas, je n'aurais eu aucun scrupule à vous emprunter un peu d'argent. A quoi serviraient donc les amis sans cela? Faites moi le plaisir d'accepter ce prêt en témoignage de bonne amitié.

A bientôt et très amicalement,
s/Jean Paul Sartre

Translation:

Simone tells me that you are temporarily without enough money. I am upset that you did not think of asking me. I assure you that, had I been in the US in the same situation, I'd have had no scruples about borrowing some money from you. What are friends good for, otherwise? Do me the favor of accepting that loan as proof of our good friendship.

13 octobre 1950 Saint Jean Cap Ferrat
Alpes Maritimes

Mon très cher Richard Wright,

Je reçois seulement votre invitation chez Jay Clifford. Vous devinez bien que si j'avais été à Paris, vous m'auriez vu, comme toujours, fidèle à votre moindre signe.

On me demande un article pour *Le Droit de Vivre* (Alliance Antiraciste). Je le voudrais important et bref. Pourriez-vous m'envoyer à Saint-Jean Cap Ferrat quelques documents sur la situation actuelle à Harlem?

De coeur à vous,
Jean Cocteau

Translation:

I just received your invitation to Jay Clifford's. You can easily guess that, had I been in Paris, you'd have seen me, as usual, faithfully ready to obey your slightest sign.

I have been asked for an article by *Le Droit de Vivre* (anti-racist alliance) I'd like it to be important and short. Could you send me to Saint Jean Cap Ferrat, a few documents on the present situation in Harlem?

21 July 1959

My dear friend,

I have read your latest book, *White Man Listen,* with the utmost interest.

Allow me first to congratulate you on your courage and clearsightedness. You have told a few healthy truths, although sometimes disagreeable ones, to Whites and Blacks alike. Both of them can accept those truths because one feels, throughout the book, a big surge of human fraternity.

I'll make one reservation only. You cannot hide your distrust of Christianity in general and Roman Catholicism in particular. I can easily account for this distrust through your situation as an American Negro, as a man of Anglo-Saxon and Protestant culture. I do not think, however, that this distrust is well-founded. The facts prove that the Catholic Church has pursued, since the Liberation (from the Germans), a strong effort towards decolonization. To such a point that a colonialist was able to call one of his books *Vatican against France.*

Of course, I am myself a Catholic and of Latin culture, which may render me partial. Yet I believe I am clearsighted enough for my partiality not to be exaggerated.

I tried to see you this year. Unluckily I am in Africa most of the time and you are not always in Paris. I hope I'll be luckier in September.

In the meantime, my Dear Friend, I remain, with great admiration, cordially yours,

s/Léopold Sédar Senghor
Président de l'Assemblée fédérale du Mali
Sénateur de la Communauté

Docteur Frantz Fanon
Hôpital Psychiatrique de Saint-Alban
(Lozère)

Saint Alban, 6 January 1953

Dear Sir,

I apologize for the freedom I take in writing to you. Alioune Diop, the editor of *Présence Africaine,* was kind enough to give me your address. I am working on a study bearing on the human breadth of your works.

Of your work I have *Native Son, Black Boy, Twelve Million Black Voices, Uncle Tom's Children* which I have ordered (I do not know whether the book is available in France), two short stories published, one in *Les Temps Modernes,* the other in *Présence Africaine.*

Eager to circumscribe in the most complete way the breadth of your message, I'd greatly appreciate your letting me know the title of those works I might be ignorant of.

My name must be unknown to you. I have written an essay *Black Skin, White Masks* which has been published by Le Seuil, in which I intended to show the systematic misunderstanding between Whites and Blacks.

Hoping to hear from you, I am, very sincerely yours,

s/Frantz Fanon

Reminiscences

WINBURN T. THOMAS

In response to my note of condolence after Richard Wright's death, his widow responded: "It seems impossible that the small urn of ash is all that is left!" Mrs. Wright knew down deep such was not the case. Dick's books, his impact on writers, of whom he was "Dean" in Paris, and friends' memories of him are Richard's perpetual memorial.

I met Richard Wright first when, having registered at the press hotel for the Bandung Conference, we were assigned to the same room. During the ten days or so of this history making event, we were together almost 24 hours daily. The refraction of the Bandung Conference through Richard's consciousness was more illuminating for me than the proceedings. The commendations I received for my in-depth interpretation in *The Christian Century* owed more to our informal evaluations than to my own perceptions. We ate at common table during the Conference with editors, broadcasters and a Congressman. After hearing the meal-time comments of professionals, Richard would say to me, "It appears that we are attending two different events."

Richard became our house guest following the Conference, during which time he wrote *The Color Curtain,* his interpretation of the Bandung Conference. I was impressed by his writing methodology. During the proceedings of the Conference he took notes which subsequently he transcribed on the typewriter. Having completed these, he then wove the total into a finished manuscript. Subsequently, when I was a guest in his apartment on the Left Bank of Paris, he was putting the finishing touches on *Pagan Spain.* He used white enamel to cover any disfiguring spots on the typescript, thus producing copy so immaculate it could have been photostated for distribution.

Richard and I carried on a friendly argument from our initial 1955 meeting until his death. He had been severe in his criticisms of missionaries—of whom I was one. While I insisted he was unnecessarily harsh, I also was forced to concede that we as a profession had been a tool of imperialism, and suffered from the racism which characterizes much of the white world. Admitting that he as an American shared some of the limitations of his own cultural background he stated, "I am a missionary to the missionaries. By my prodding, perhaps you will face up to the implications of what you do. You give Third World peoples a vision of social justice and liberation, then when they seek these ends by violence, you repudiate them, insisting this is not what you had intended."

One of his shortcomings which I spelled out to Richard was that despite his blackness, he had behaved in Africa as a typical Yankee. Prior to our meeting Richard had written *Black Power*, a study of Kwame Nkrumah. In planning a trip to Ghana I requested introductions from Richard, one of whom proved to be a professor at the University. This professor subsequently invited me to attend some of his seminars, at one of which the students examined *Black Power.* They insisted that Dick had failed to understand them, that he had lived as an American, and that he had worn the passé pith-helmet. "While we accepted him initially because he was black, we soon discovered he was not one of us," was one comment. When I reported this to Richard, he laughed and admitted he was a westerner after all.

During my visit in his Paris apartment, Richard insisted that I visit Spain, which he had treated in his most recent book. "As a Christian missionary, you should see for yourself," he insisted, "the plight of the white negroes—the Protestants of Iberia." At his insistence I changed my return routing to Asia so as to visit Madrid, where I discovered that his analysis was indeed correct. He who made no Christian pretensions, was nevertheless sensitive to the frustrations and discriminations suffered by a minority people. Thanks to Richard, I gained an understanding of a situation which has conditioned my interpretation of Pagan Spain's culture.

Richard Wright was no ivory tower philosopher. While some have criticized him for "remaining in the splendid isolation of Paris" rather than identifying himself with the civil rights struggle in the USA, he was finding causes in Paris with which he could identify. One night, he and I went pub-crawling on the Left Bank, talking with Algerian revolutionaries. His ready wit, his free use of French, and his blackness enabled him to enter into dialogue with these victims of French colonialism. Their cause had become his cause.

Mrs. Wright was a beautiful Brooklyn girl of Polish ancestry. His two daughters were reared in an environment free of the restraints he had experienced as recorded in *Black Boy.* When I was staying with them in 1958, his sixteen year old daughter received word of her acceptance to Cambridge—an accomplishment which would have been denied her had she been a product of Mississippi schools.

During the month he was writing *The Color Curtain,* sharing the lower bunk of a double decker with one of my sons, Pan American Airlines dumped on my doorstep an unknown and unexpected touring college student from the USA. There was no alternative but to remove the other son from the bed, and put him on a pallet, so that the reservation-less Caucasian could sleep. It developed that the college student was from Jackson, Mississippi, where Richard had spent his childhood. I suspect that when the boy returned home, he did not advertise that he had been compelled by circumstances to share a bed with a black from the same city.

HORACE CAYTON and SIDNEY WILLIAMS
(from a tape recording made in August, 1967)

"Well, Horace, I think Dick went to Africa with a point of view or a frame of reference that was basically American, or western. And you may recall his experience on that boat, the things he reported on the trip on the boat from London—his conversations and his experience with this African traveller. In that he reveals his—well, I don't like to use the word 'limitation,' and yet I don't know any other way."

"Well, after all, Dick wasn't God."

"Dick was not God? But no. This is in no way an attempt to detract from him, Horace; I'm merely trying to put him in proper perspective in reference to this African experience."

"Sidney, did he feel that he was sufficiently important, so that if DuBois was invited surely Dick Wright should be invited?"

"He didn't verbalise it, but somehow or other I got that impression because of his intense curiosity and concern about our going down. I think, Horace, that with about fifty black American personalities going down to Ghana for this occasion, headed, although he was not able to go, by Dr. DuBois, I sort of think that Dick felt that he belonged in that group."

"Did he make any reference to Nkrumah?"

"No, not to my recollection."

"Because he didn't get along with them?"

"No, Horace, he didn't make any reference to Nkrumah in Paris in '57 when we were going through. His thought was on Dr. DuBois and whether or not he was going to be able to go."

"Did he express any opinion about DuBois?"

"Yes, he did. Now, let me see if I can recall. He was championing Dr. DuBois' cause."

"And what was Dr. DuBois' cause?"

"I'm trying to remember, Horace, whether or not it had to do with his arrest in Washington . . . I'm not sure, I wish my memory were better."

"That's all right, Sidney, all these pieces will tie in."

"Horace, he had a deep concern there about Dr. DuBois. And that is one of the primary reasons for his wanting me to see this French writer, Guerin, because seemingly he and Dick had had considerable conversation about whether or not Dr. DuBois was going to be able to go, and whether or not Dr DuBois was justified in his criticism of America that got him into this difficulty with the State Department. Now I don't remember too much about that, do you? Except it was to do with the peace group that was going to meet up in the Scandinavian countries."

"Stockholm, I think it was."

"Yes, that sort of comes to mind."

"A meeting of all the peace forces in Stockholm. And you see Shirley DuBois, she was born in Seattle. . . . But, now, did Dick accept DuBois as sort of the leader of Pan-Africanism?"

"Yes."

"Because the people didn't like Dick to accept anybody . . ."

"Well, I can see that too, but I would certainly deduce from my contacts with him there in late February, 1957, on our way to Ghana that he was looking upon Dr. DuBois as the real patriarch of the cause, not only of the Black Americans, but of African Independence. . . ."

"Sid, we mentioned this once before: it's *my* opinion, and I don't want to put it on you, but in later years Dick missed America, and perhaps he would have come back if he could have done so gracefully. . . ."

"Dick was the leader of the black American community in Paris at that time. All reference was, shall we say, to him. Whatever his position was on anything that came up of mutual concern was the position of the group. There may be a few that differed with him, but without doubt he was the patriarch of the group, he was the leader."

"Did you get the feeling that he was at home, and happy?"

"No, Horace. But that is not an easy question to answer. While he enjoyed complete acceptance among the French intellectuals, Dick was not wholly and completely satisfied with his life in France."

"Now what is the evidence?"

"Number one, he sent his older daughter back to England, you may recall, to school. Now that, to me, is significant. If he had decided to become a French citizen, if he had decided to become French, that would hardly be the kind of educational experience he would want his daughter subjected to. He would want her to become French. Then, the next thing—I think Dick made some reference—when he went to England and wanted to see her, maybe when he was thinking of moving over there, he was treated most rudely by the British authorities. And I think he was hurt by that experience. And I got the impression that Dick felt that that treatment he was subjected to by the British authorities was not necessarily one pure and wholly British, but that the British were doing this at the suggestion of Washington."

"Was it his notion that Washington wanted him to come back to the United States?"

"Yeah."

"Did he voice this in any way?"

"Yes, Horace. What he had to say about this black agent who was over there and giving them a lot of trouble, harrassing them in one way or another. That stated it pretty well."

"I've talked to some, like Ken Kinnamon down in Illinois, who wrote his doctor's dissertation on him at Harvard. And he advanced the notion that Dick, towards the end, was becoming pretty paranoic. And his pre-occupation with this black spy . . ."

"I don't think that was any paranoid action, Horace. My knowledge of the operation of the CIA, based on my own experience, in Africa in particular, during the war and subsequently, would lead me to believe that this concern that he and I had . . . wasn't something from the excitement of one's imagination. It was real, quite real."

"Now you said he was the leader of the black writers. Did you hear any stories about him?"

"No, I don't recall any stories; I may have heard some but they have eluded me now. What I heard from all these fellows was something that you could sum up in one word—respect."

"What do you mean?"

"By that I mean that Dick was very young but they had a high respect and regard for him. I don't know any other way to put it. It was almost the kind of devotion and respect that a devout Catholic would have for a priest. Or the kind of thing I saw in England on my first trip abroad in 1936. A group of Americans, we were walking through Hyde Park being escorted by a British anthropologist, and one of these inept Americans made some comment about Wally Simpson and the Prince of Wales. I expected a rather casual kind of flippant remark to come from him, this Britisher, about Wally Simpson and the Prince, and he shocked all of us, shocked me, too, knowing him to be a socialist, when he turned to this American girl who raised the question and said to her, 'We Britishers do not discuss the Royal Family with any foreigners.' . . ."

Heartblow

A Sequence for Richard Wright

MICHAEL S. HARPER

I. RAT FEVER: HISTORY AS HALLUCINATION

A man's a man
when he can kill
rats with bare hands,
eat them
or be eaten by them.

Tracked leavings
on the village roof,
out the window
sewers overflowing;
a man's a man
when he can eat himself up
and leave no tracks.

II. NEAR THE WHITE HOUSE

A cross is a machine
in a ship's hull,
an anchor on the Potomac
is a mansion.
This black statue curtseys
in a vanilla smile,
its lips a cross
burning, its heat
flicking the mansion lights;
beacons on the marbleheads
and a sorrow song is a cross

III. THE MEANING OF PROTEST

Between the world and me
a black boy is a native
son with a long dream
if a white man will listen.
Uncle Tom's children
were eight men, all outsiders,
fish bellies living
underground.

Pagan Spain taught us the church
was woman as mystery, a penis
the sword to butcher each other;
Black Power! we're not going
to the moon, and in Bandung
white man can't come,
he's on a savage holiday.

Blossoms in a peanut field
won't bring me home;
something in the hum
of cotton is a glue
that won't hold red soil still;
ten million voices spliced
on an iron cross
between the world, and me, and you.

IV. TREE FEVER

Skin of trees cut down;
men in trees,
sacks of scrotum
breastmeat on brims,
soldier hats
on each father patroller,
posse the flag on picnic
their stars and stripes
our skin of scars.

V. BIGGER'S BLUES

In this case
Mary's mama is correspondent:
blind witch with threaded
needles on the family table.
Ping-pong money to the poor.
Poor Mary gone off C.O.D.
in a golden trunk
head handed to her.
At the furnace where Bigger
hatted up, mama's
touching led him crazy
(what begins with N
and rhymes with Bigger)
on, on, on.

VI. PARABLE

Black-stemmed ax
stuck in white tree;
roots in waterhole
roped underground
get tree fever;
cut off handle,
tree die.

VII. HISTORY AS DIABOLICAL MATERNALISM

When I grind glass
I think of lenses
swallowed like sugar,
a preacher with glass eye,
a eunuch named Jesus,
Black Mary in his cottonfield.

VIII. HEARTBLOW: MESSAGES

I sit in cubbyhole,
wasp nests north and south,
woods to the west, ocean east,
the highway north a southern road.
Goggle-eyed lamplights
blink uneven wattage
as the pulses
of your soulful heart.

I met a man who gave you bread
and meat and a warm bed
while you wrote *Black Boy,*
another who shared your Chicago loft;
some wait for released papers,
some salve old photographs.

A campus librarian near
Hollywood reads the unread
books to move with Bigger,
sees Mary's spittle as sperm
pushing her trunk,
holds the body as you hack her neck,
watches Bessie's downdraft
as a cross-corner shot.

That parable of black man, white woman,
the man's penis slung to his shin,
erect, foaming, in that woman's womb,
the ambivalent female with a smirk-shriek,
daylights of coitus stuck together,
through the nights the razored solution;
that the black man is nature,
the woman, on her drilled pedestal, divine,
the man with razor an artisan
in symmetry steel and sharp blades—
let him melt into his vat of precious metal,

let the female wipe her face of sperm,
let the black man's penis shrink to normal
service, let the posse eat their whips instead.

On the Seine I thought of you
on the towpath to Notre Dame;
at the Blue Note looking for Bud
on his parisian thorofare;
caught your blues from black musicians
while you died alone in prose;
some said you'd died of disconnection;
souls said you dealt your own heartblow.

IX. SPIRITUAL

grandma's picket fence
balloon mask dancing
bloody moon your black ribcage.

X. AFTERWORD: A FILM

Erect in the movies
with a new job,
Trader Horn
and *The Gay Woman*
unfold in a twinbill:
drums, wild dancing,
naked men, the silver
veils on the South Side.
He imagines nothing:
it is all before him,
born in a dream:
a gorilla broke loose
from his zoo
in a tuxedo: baboon.
You pick your red bottom.
The Daltons are the movies.

On my wall are pictures:
Jack Johnson, Joe Louis,
Harlow and Rogers:
"see the white god and die."

Underground I live in veils,
brick and cement,
the confession beaten out,
slung with hung carcasses,
a bloody cleaver grunting,
a dead baby in the sewer:
"all the people I saw were guilty."

Marked black I was shot,
double-conscious brother in the veil—
without an image of act or thought
double-conscious brother in the veil—

The rape: "Mrs. Dalton, it's me,
Bigger, I've brought Miss Dalton
home and she's drunk:"
to be the idea in these minds,
double-conscious brother in the veil—
father and leader where is my king,
veils of kingship will lead these folks
double-conscious brother in the veil—
"see the white gods and die"
double-conscious brother in the veil—

Some Critical Commentary

Bessie's Blues

EDWARD A. WATSON

Although *Native Son* encompasses a multifaceted attack on almost every American cultural stereotype, from the impersonality of the big-business machinery of ghetto real-estate to frenetic cross-burning Klansmen, from the blind altruism of the millionaire philanthropic "liberal" to the knife-wielding darkie, no reference is made to jazz or jazz-oriented music throughout the entire novel. Once, during Bigger's self-searching conversation with Boris Max in the Cook County jail, where he tries to explain the very tenuous nature of his early church affiliation, is some mention made of the Negro's escape into music:

> "Did you ever go to church, Bigger?"
> "Yeah; when I was little. But that was a long time ago."
> "Your folks were religious?"
> "Yeah; they went to church all the time."
> "Why did you stop going?"
> "I didn't like it. There was nothing in it. As, all they did was sing and shout and pray all the time. And it didn't get 'em nothing. All the colored folks do that, but it don't get 'em nothing. The white folks got everything" *(Native Son,* Harper and Row, Paperback edition, p. 329).

On two other occasions Wright mentions music or singing: when he returns home to get his gun on the first day, Bigger hears his mother singing: "Lord, I want to be a Christian, / In my heart, in my heart. . . ." And at Ernie's Kitchen Shack, "Somebody put a nickel in an automatic phonograph and they listened to the music."

The lack of reference to music, dancing, inherent rhythm, and the hand-clapping soul-searing hymn-singing of the Negro seems odd in a book of the calibre of *Native Son* which explores and explodes all of the stereotypes of the Negro held by white America. However, it seems that Wright achieved a subtle yet powerful imaginative success through Bessie Mears, Bigger's girl, whose speech and life-style embodies in no simple way the spirit of the *blues.*

Unlike Mrs. Thomas, whose medium of escape from the trials of life is religion, Bessie's anodyne is alcohol and sex. Except that she is Bigger's girl, there is nothing special about Bessie: she works as a maid in a white neighborhood, is easily coaxed into compromises by the scent of money, loves her "no-good" man, and delights in the passionate euphoria of sex. Nevertheless, when she speaks, there always emerges that incredulous, searching pessimism of the forlorn heroine whom the *blues* apotheosizes. Her two plaintive "songs" on pages 169-170 and 215-216 are, in my estimation, literary variations on the extemporaneous blues shout.

The first speech which Bessie "sings" immediately after Bigger confesses to having murdered Mary Dalton is fraught with the despair, fear, and pain of the lost lover implicated in guilt by association:

> "Bigger, please! Don't do this to me! Please! All I do is work, work like a dog! From morning till night. I ain't got no happiness. I ain't never had none. I ain't got nothing and you do this to me. After how good I been to you. Now you just spoil my whole life. I've done everything for you I know how and you do this to me. *Please,* Bigger. . . ." She turned her head and stared at the floor. "Lord, don't let this happen to me! I ain't done nothing for this to come to me! I just work! I ain't had no happiness, no nothing. I just work. I'm black and I work and don't bother nobody. . . ."

Clearly, Bessie's blues are an extension of the earthly complaint in the tradition of Ma Rainey and Bessie Smith. The elements of jazz lyrics prior to 1930 were more cynical and distrusting, and specifically condemned those motivated by self-interest—usually, the hard-hearted lover (male or female) —who ran roughshod over the less fortunate partner. In this respect, Wright probably looked back to Bessie Smith and Ma Rainey rather than to Billie Holiday who, singing between 1936 and 1939, came more directly under the influence of the optimistic lyricism of Tin Pan Alley. The gulf between "Sing Sing Blues," "Sinful Blues," and "Bleeding Hearted Blues" (Bessie Smith) and "A Sailboat in the Moonlight," "The Man I Love" and "Yesterdays"—("Yesterdays, Yesterdays,/ Days I knew as happy, sweet, sequestered days,/ Olden days, golden days,/ Days of mad romance and love") by Billie Holiday, is rather extreme and points to a decreasing emphasis of the elements of fear, pain and brutality of the earlier blues. Wright, of course, was concerned with exactly that fear, pain, and brutality which is the logical consequence of the dehumanization of the black man. Hence, Bessie's *blues* is a poignant reminder of the suffering woman caught up in the web of uncontrollable destructive forces.

With something akin to both editorial and poetic license, I have attempted to reconstruct Bessie's first speech into a medium which, more or less, approximates the more traditional and extemporaneous blues voice:

BESSIE'S BLUES #1

[Lover,] please! Don't do this to me! Please!
All I do is work, work like a dog!
From morning till night.
I ain't got no happiness, I ain't never had none,
I ain't got nothing and you do this to me
After how good I been to you.

Now you just spoil my whole life
[And] I've done everything for you I know how,
And you do this to me;
Please, [Lover] . . .
[I ain't done nothing for this to come to me.]

Lord [up above], don't let this happen to me!
['Cause] I ain't done nothing for this to come to me!
I just work, [work like a dog];
I ain't had no happiness, no nothing
[And I ain't never had none],
I just work, [work like a dog];
[For] I'm black and I work and don't bother nobody.

[Lord up above, don't let this happen to me,
Lord up above, don't let this happen to me. . . .]

All the traditional elements are here: hard-hearted lover, lack of worldly goods, lack of happiness, hard work, comparison to a dog, the "sin" of blackness, docility, and the appeal to God. Bessie's first *blues* is conditioned by both fear and despair and results in an aching consciousness summing up the brutal experience of her life.

The second speech which appears on pages 215 and 216 is much longer than the first and adds two additional dimensions to the first *blues*: flight from justice (which, in *Native Son* is synonymous with death) and recognition of fate. Bessie speaks:

> "Oh Lord," she moaned. "What's the use of running. They'll catch us anywhere. I should've known this would happen." She clenched her hands in front of her and rocked to and fro with her eyes closed upon gushing tears. "All my life's been full of hard trouble. If I wasn't hungry, I was sick. And if I wasn't sick, I was in trouble. I ain't never bothered nobody. I just worked hard everyday as long as I can remember, till I was tired enough to drop; then I had to get drunk to forget it. I had to get drunk to sleep. That's all I ever did. And now I'm in this. They looking for me and when they catch me they'll kill me." She bent her head to the floor. "God only knows why I ever let you treat me this way. I wish to God I never seen you. I wish one of us had died before we was born. God knows I do! All you ever caused me was trouble. All you ever did since we been knowing each other was to get me drunk so's you could have me. That was all! I see it now. I ain't drunk now. I see everything you ever did to me. I didn't want to see it before. I was too busy thinking about how good I felt when I was with you. I thought I was happy, but deep down in me I knew I wasn't. But you got me into this murder and I see it all now. I been a fool, just a blind dumb black drunk fool. Now I got to run away and I know deep down in your heart you really don't care."

This speech is more intense and revealing than the first, and, in keeping with traditional blues, reveals a pathetic autobiography which is flashed across a screen, as it were, in a moment of personal catastrophe. Here, nothing is tragic; there is no resolution. Bessie's confession is a confession of failure, and she has no hope of conquering life since she has not really lived.

For purposes of upholding the structural divisions of the novel, I have divided this second speech into two *blues,* the first of which contemplates the inevitability of death despite attempts to flee (Flight), and the second, the fateful consequences of Bessie's association with her hard-hearted lover (Fate). Thus, the three songs which Bessie sings correspond with, and form a counterpoint to the three divisions of the book—Fear, Flight, Fate. Admittedly, I have forced the speeches to fit a pre-established structural pattern; nevertheless, the point to be made is that the "songs" treat characteristic blues themes which fall naturally under the three divisions of the book. Again, with some license, I have *constructed* Bessie's Blues #2:

> Oh, Lord, what's the use of running?
> They'll catch us anywhere;
> I should've known this would happen.
> (Repeat)
>
> All my life's been full of hard trouble:
> If I wasn't hungry, I was sick
> And if I wasn't sick, I was in trouble.
> I ain't never bothered nobody,
> I just worked hard every day
> (As long as I can remember)
> Till I was tired enough to drop.
> Then I had to get drunk to forget it,
> I had to get drunk to sleep;
> That's all I ever did
>
> And now I'm in this.
> They looking for me
> And when they catch me they'll kill me.
>
> [Oh, Lord, what's the use of running
> Oh, Lord, what's the use of running. . . .]

Bessie's anguish is not directed to Bigger but to an inscrutable God who Bigger, at a later moment, believes is capable of creating an "obscene joke" on the black man. Bessie's confession is to an implacable God and she senses doom with the extreme conviction of the pessimist. Part of the *pathos* of the *blues* is its recurring sense of doom. The speaker always recognizes the conflict between life and death but is powerless to guide the self into any alternate condition which even vaguely suggests a promise of Life. In short, the *blues* is a futile gasp in time, a perpetual and unredeeming sorrow. (The current practice of singing *spirituals* with the intonations and tonalities of the *blues* is an attempt, conscious or unconscious, to fuse two philosophically incompatible complaints.) This sense of futility is carried over into the third song where Bessie sees the culmination of her life etched in sharp strokes of blackness:

BESSIE'S BLUES #3

God only knows why I ever let you treat me this way;
I wish to God I had never seen you.
I wish one of us had died before we was born
God knows I do.

All you ever caused me was trouble
Just plain black trouble;
All you ever did since we been knowing each other
Was to get me drunk so's you could have me.
That was all; I see it now. . . .

But I ain't drunk now,
I see everything you ever did to me;
I didn't want to see it before
['Cause] I was busy thinking
How good I felt when I was with you.

I thought I was happy
But deep down in me, I knew I wasn't
But you got me in this [thing] murder,
[And I see it all now].

I been a fool,
Just a blind dumb black drunk fool
Now I got to run away and I know
Deep down in your heart
You really don't care.

[I see it now,
I see it all now,
God knows I do
'Cause deep down in your heart
You really don't care.]

Bessie's recognition of her plight must be seen as the final step to oblivion from the release of her meaningless life. Her life has been spent in toil, an unrelenting pain which is only momentarily relieved by drink. Even sex, we now discover, had no real meaning for her. (This fact is further substantiated when Bigger rapes her before he kills her.) Now, when she recognizes that the man she loves "really don't care," life is over for her, and the *blues* is her testimony that she paid her dues. Bessie's song recalls all of the forlorn sentiments of the blues singer, and her wailing is the private anguish of the self as scapegoat.

There is some possibility that Wright avoided the explicit in depicting the *blues* because he recognized it as the subtle art it is. And since *Native Son* treated all the prejudices, stereotypes and cultural prejudgments as art, it seems only fitting that Wright should have treated the blues as a very sensitive and vibrant art form. In this sense, *Native Son* is one extended blues the spirit of which is particularized in Bessie. Wright chose Bessie, perhaps because of another soulful Bessie, and, perhaps, because she was the only black woman in the novel who could sing of broken hearts and broken dreams, of Fear and Flight and Fate; of a life full of "just plain black trouble."

The Long Dream

KATHERINE SPRANDEL

Throughout his career Richard Wright drew on his Southern childhood to give vitality and meaning to his work. In his first novel as well as his last, it is possible to discover references to Wright's own life. *Black Boy,* the record of Wright's youth, contains the sources of much of his thinking. A bittersweet account of his Mississippi years, it ranges from Whitmanesque rhapsodies to impassioned denunciations of black values and aspirations. In it Wright chronicles his love-hatred of his world and his struggles to come to terms with himself. Years later, in *The Long Dream,* he was again to write of a young hero whose initiation closely resembled his own.

This theme of initiation is strong in American letters, ranging from Hawthorne's "My Kinsman, Major Molineux" through Farrell's *Studs Lonigan.* But initiation, although it brings knowledge, does not necessarily bring acceptance. As Ihab Hassan notes in *Radical Innocence,* initiation in America has moved steadily toward victimization and renunciation. Out of this obverse initiation arises the rebel-victim, the outraged hero "on trial for nothing less than his *being.*" (*Radical Innocence* [New York, 1966], pp. 34f and 60.)

The black man in America is a paradigm of the innocent hero victimized by a guilty society. Traditionally the end of a black youth's initiation has been renunciation: the white majority society rejects him, and he in turn isolates himself from the rest of the world, for all practical purposes recognizing and accepting his inferiority. Deep within, however, stirs the wrath of a violated man. This anger smolders in the pages of *Lawd*

Today and sears the pages of *Native Son.* A similar rage to live in freedom drives Cross Damon to violence in *The Outsider.* But it isn't until *The Long Dream* that he gives us a fictional character who can explain the alienation and violence of his earlier characters. This novel presents the initiation rituals of Fishbelly Tucker in Clintonville, Mississippi. Drawn from Wright's own childhood, the book recalls *Black Boy* and clarifies the motives driving Bigger Thomas and Cross Damon, both of whom also grew up in the South.

Philosophically the book is much less complicated than either *Native Son* or *The Outsider.* But, although the first part, "Daydreams and Nightmares," builds with almost painful slowness, it does delineate clearly Fish's first experiences with the three important elements of his initiation: whites, police, and women. Furthermore, in this section, Wright establishes the central relationship between father and son: ironically, it is Tyree, the loving father, who helps destroy his son.

Wright, it has been suggested, has developed the strong and strangely admirable Tyree in an attempt to create in his fiction the father image that he lacked in his life. Unscrupulous and clever, Tyree is passionately involved with the happiness of his son, unlike Wright's own father who deserted his family. Having mastered the art of accommodation, Tyree plays the fool and profits from prejudice. His deception catches up with him after the Grove fire when he is unable to convince the police chief that he will not implicate him. In fear, Cantley kills him. Before Tyree dies, however, he teaches Fish his most galling lesson: to co-exist with whites a black must surrender his manhood.

The fact that blacks cooperated with whites to unman their youth incensed Wright, who himself refused the advice of his childhood friends to act like an Uncle Tom. In *The Long Dream* the father himself encourages his son's disordered personality. This seemingly self-defeating treatment is the black's pragmatic response to an uncompromising situation. Edward Bland calls the condition that this treatment creates "pre-individualism." Drawing on Bland's theory, Ralph Ellison explains in *Shadow and Act* that this pre-individual state is induced artificially through taboos and violence in order to "impress the Negro child with the omniscience and omnipotence of the whites." *(Shadow and Act* [New York, 1964], p. 95.)

But as surely as black parents act to destroy, they act to save. As John Williams points out in his introduction to *Sissie,* blacks "love their children as much as any others . . . But because they are black the parental burden is greater." *(Sissie* [Garden City, 1969], pp. ix-x.) When Wright censures his own people he is only too aware, as he points out in *Black Boy,* that they have been excluded from the benefits of Western culture and its traditions. How black parents react may be deplorable, but it is certainly understandable, at times even necessary for the survival of their children.

In an attempt to explain Fish's alienation from other blacks, Wright thoroughly examines the boy's relationship with them. Early in the book we learn that Fish is not allowed to associate with the black railroad workers because, although they are his color, they are not his kind. His father, a successful undertaker, has risen above the rest of the blacks and consequently teaches his son a certain intraracial superiority. The shame of it, however, is that Fish is left with no people to call his own. Too proud and rich to befriend the ordinary blacks and racially unable to fraternize with the whites, he is left virtually isolated.

The isolation motif assumes a new twist in Chapter 6 when Aggie West, a homosexual, is taunted and beaten by Fish's gang because he is different. Immediately after driving him off, the boys uneasily realize that they have treated Aggie just as the whites treat them. As usual, Fish represses this kind of suffering, preferring instead to live on the surface of things.

Similarly, the female sex baffles Fish as much as Aggie has. When he is seven he is totally mystified to see his father copulating with a stranger. All he learns is that his father is a magnificent liar. Later, a white whore tries to seduce him and a rather unusual woman has an orgasm on the street when the boys scare her.

But Fish's most impressive initiation with women comes vicariously to him through Chris, the black bellboy at a local hotel. When Chris is betrayed by a white prostitute who tires of his sexual services, the blacks of Clintonville fear for their lives. Tyree refers to a possible race war. He is so concerned for his son's safety that he turns Chris' brutal murder into an object lesson for Fish. Father and son witness the gruesome autopsy after Chris has been castrated and horribly beaten. By destroying his body the whites have avenged the white girl. On a more positive note, because Chris has died for them, the blacks will have a period of reprieve from the whites. It is therefore relatively easy for the doctor and the undertaker to be calm during the autopsy, both having accepted life on the whites' terms.

But Tyree, pragmatic as he is, grieves over the black man's condition. Echoing the book's title, he laments, "A black man's a dream, son, a dream that can't come true." He expands this concept through further advice, "Dream, Fish. But be careful what you dream. Dream only what can happen." (*The Long Dream* [New York: Ace Publishing Corporation, 1958], p. 73. Hereafter all page references to this work appear in parentheses in the text.) Despite his father's counsel, Fish's own dream of life will end in tragedy and flight. Although Fish does not consciously grasp the significance of Chris' death, enough fragments of the experience linger to reinforce the taboo of the white woman.

The police offer Fish further insights into his position as a black man when they arrest him on a petty trespassing charge. In a sporting mood, they threaten to castrate him with a penknife. Terrified, Fish faints—to the delight of his tormentors.

When Tyree visits him in jail, Fish is sickened to see his beloved father acting like a black fool. Searching himself for the meaning of what he has seen, Fish recognizes with a jolt that his father has tricked the white man into letting him go. He also realizes that any Uncle Tom can manipulate the whites. And so it seems that Fish himself begins his "act" when he leaves jail in a shuffling gait, the figure of a docile black boy.

Having been threatened by the police and disappointed by his father, Fish heads home. On the way, he discovers a badly injured dog. In a conscious effort to prepare himself for death, he swiftly eviscerates the animal. Wright's imagery is particularly effective here as he allows the act to convey the emotion.

As Fish's world closes in, determining his fate as an outsider, he looks to his father for guidance. But Tyree, having accommodated himself to whites, cannot understand his rebellious son. Loving him, trying to get his mind off the whites, he innocently takes Fish to a cathouse, only to find that his son, hooked on the sweetness of sex, is then irrevocably drawn to the forbidden white woman.

Part II of the novel, "Days and Nights," revolves around the book's major themes: Fish's love-hatred of the white world and its misuse of him; his isolation from his own people; and, the transfer of a legacy from Tyree to Fish. To pacify his desires for white women, Fish, like his father before him, takes a pale mulatto mistress. Although he loves her, he abhors her acceptance of her isolation. In contrast, Fish agonizes over his own attraction to the white world and its rejection of him.

Fish's sense of isolation from blacks dominates the scenes where he collects the rent from Tyree's black tenants. He remarks to his father that the blacks are "sick" because they complain about oppression but do not act to end it. Tyree tells him to forget them. But Fish cannot, as he continues to discover the blacks' hidden hopes and obvious failures. Ultimately he reckons them parasites. He feels superior to them, unaware that his white outlook has scarred his black life; he cannot join the black community because he is enticed by the white power structure. Fish is "fatally in love with the white world, because the white world could offer him the chance to develop his personality and his wealth without fear of reprisal." (Russell Carl Brignano, *Richard Wright: An Introduction to the Man and His Works* [Pittsburgh, 1970], p. 44.) Wanting independence himself, he cannot help but desire complete freedom for self-direction, a state reserved for whites only.

To survive the anguish of collecting rent, Fish hardens himself, becoming, like his father, a façade of a man. He wears a fixed smile to cover his cynicism. He submerges his inner self; and, although he is aware of his isolation, he "acts" like a member of the community. He learns to play the nigger role. (Cross Damon also played this role well when he applied for

Lionel Lane's birth certificate in *The Outsider.)*

Fish learns how a black man must behave, when Tyree performs the Uncle Tom role expected of him by Chief Cantley. But Fish fights this role. Several nights after the great fire, Fish endures his Gethsemane, denying his identity of victim—of nigger. This mental agony, according to John Williams, is the inheritance of the black man: "to be black is to be forever embattled not only with the world of the whites, but with one's self." *(Sissie,* p. x.) Fish's internal conflict revolves around his intuition that whites are right, blacks are inferior. He, therefore, rejects them as repulsive. Unable, on the other hand to delude himself with the vision of respectability among whites, he concedes his isolation.

The first step he takes in his new struggle against the white world that has killed his father is to break with his mother. To fight the enemy he must become a man, a free man. And yet he "was with the enemy against his own people" while hating "that enemy because he saw himself and his people as the enemy saw them" (288f). Cursed with ambivalence, he is forever stranded between the two worlds.

The final section of the book, "Waking Dream," reveals this isolation. The lonely father is reincarnated in the son. As the first section was Fish's initiation and the second his probation, the third is his total victimization. He is society's child, playing the role society dictates but forbidden entry into its coveted demesne. And society demands that he, a Negro in Mississippi, be a victim. To survive, Fish plays his role just as Tyree for years had played his.

Fishbelly's attempt to accommodate himself to the white world is a miserable failure. He mimics the Uncle Tom his father had played, but it does not work for him. Eventually to save and renew his life, he flees to France. Donald Gibson finds this resolution "retrogressive": "he returns to his starting point, to 'Big Boy Leaves Home,' to the most basic and least conscious response to fear precipitated by confrontation with convention, flight." ("Richard Wright and the Tyranny of Convention," *CLA Journal,* XII [June 1969], 356f.) But for Fish, flight is his only alternative since he lacks both the friends and the self-confidence that would help him fight for manhood.

In running to France he denies his world, a world that had "emotionally crucified him" (350). But he also acts in faith. His sweetest dream is, after all, that of becoming a person, one welcomed by other human beings, although Tyree would probably have discouraged this dream as too impractical. Wright in his final book is thus protesting "against the injustice that destroys [a man's] spirit, crushes his dignity." (Edward Margolies, *The Art of Richard Wright* [Carbondale, 1969], p. 151.)

The tragedy of Fishbelly Tucker is not his running to France, but his ruined potential. Reasonably intelligent, endowed with his father's native cunning, and overly sensitive, Fish is at the mercy of his environment (as is Studs Lonigan). Even as an adolescent, Fishbelly could grasp the real significance of Tyree's acting, Chris' death, his own identity crisis. But his sensitivity has been his Achilles' heel. Easily hurt, he could tolerate neither the whites' brutalities nor their subtleties. Instead of reaching out to others, Fish has rapidly learned to focus on himself. Becoming so sensitive to his own needs and desires that he lives solely for himself, he is warped: he fears and envies the whites, and scorns and exploits the blacks. Simultaneously, however, he abhors his situation and himself, craving friends and understanding. He tries to retain his self-esteem and manhood but is forced to surrender them to survive. Because he is sensitive, he continually resents his inferior status and the necessity for role playing, realizing that no man should have to buy his life with his castration. Fish is an unwilling victim, a man on the prowl to regain selfhood.

As a result, by the end of the book, Fishbelly Tucker, isolate and victimized non-man, has begun the existential search for self. Through the rituals of sacrifice, sex, and defeat, Fish's initiation has resulted in alienation. He has been on trial for his very being. The knowledge initiation brings is that he must flee if he hopes to achieve self-individuation, since the blacks and whites have an unspoken pact to destroy Fish's personality. The results of this destruction are evident in *Native Son* and *The Outsider,* whose heroes take other paths to combat the state of selflessness.

In *Native Son* Wright has created a proletarian novel that protests the social and environmental determinism of Bigger Thomas in a capitalistic society. And yet he deftly moves his hero out of the strictures of naturalism into the freedom of existentialism. After demonstrating that whites are responsible for making Bigger an outlaw and finally a murderer, Wright lifts Bigger out of this morass, permitting him to make an existential decision. Rejecting the necessity of scapegoats, Bigger accepts himself for what he is, a murderer, an identity which he embraces after being invisible for twenty years. Although he dies victorious, he dies alone: his crime and identity have condemned him to social alienation.

The existentialism evident in "The Man Who Lived Underground" and at the end of *Native Son* is simply a preview of that in *The Outsider,* the novel Richard Lehan calls "the most express treatment of the existential theme in American fiction." ("Existentialism in Recent American Fiction: The Demonic Quest," *Recent American Fiction*, ed. Joseph Waldmeir [Boston, 1963], p. 74.) But by the end of this book Wright has discarded both communism and existentialism, concluding on notes of dismay and disgust.

Since Wright has already written off religion, when he rejects the existential position, he is left with the rather vague and untenable philosophy of love. Where this takes him is obvious in *The Long Dream*: Fish was initially ruined by his father's overly protective love; Fish further destroyed himself through his own love of the white world and its temptations. Therefore, when he saves his life by escaping to France, he has no concrete ideas of how to either accept his past or love himself. As early as his childhood Wright could find little love in his own people, and he surely found little in whites. It is not surprising, then, although it is disappointing, that Wright leaves his last hero literally up in the air.

All his life Richard Wright protested against the dehumanizing conditions the black man lived under. This passionate concern with the welfare of his people led Wright to communism in the thirties and existentialism in the fifties;

neither philosophy satisfied him. Perhaps this is why Wright spent the last months of his life intrigued with the mysteries of the Orient. The knowledge of the West that his own initiation disclosed triggered his exceptional novels, but it hardly brought him peace. In the work of an honest artist, one can hardly expect to find answers when none exist.

Wright, Baldwin, Cleaver

MORRIS DICKSTEIN

Irving Howe has written that "the day *Native Son* appeared American culture was changed forever . . . it made impossible a repetition of the old lies. . . . Richard Wright's novel brought out into the open, as no one ever had before, the hatred, fear and violence that have crippled and may yet destroy our culture." Well, American culture is an elephantine thing, hard to change with a novel. But the consciousness of blacks themselves was indeed altered, and surely no black writer could ever tell himself the old lies. Whatever the later attacks on Wright, his work became an effective north star of Negro writing, which helped his successors to find their own directions.

Attacked, abandoned as a literary example by Baldwin and Ellison, whose early work he had typically encouraged, he has now become, after long eclipse and a decade after his death, the favored ancestor of a great many new black writers, who reject his successors and feel much akin to his militant spirit. Parricide, after all, is one of the quicker methods of succession, and nothing can more conveniently legitimate the bloody deed than an appeal to the authority of the grandfather, himself the previous victim.

It would be superficial, however, to think that Baldwin alone killed Richard Wright until the angry sixties came along to resurrect him. In some sense Wright's kind of novel was already dying or dead by the time he found it. In *Black Boy* Wright describes the impact of reading Dreiser for the first time: "I was overwhelmed. . . . It would have been impossible for me to have told anyone what I derived from these novels, for it was nothing else than a sense of life itself. All my life had shaped me for the realism, the naturalism of the modern novel." How quaint the last phrase must have seemed in the late forties and fifties, when the modern novel meant the modernist novel, when everyone knew without reading him that Dreiser was crude and vulgar compared to James, when, increasingly, the only modern American classics in fiction were Hemingway, Faulkner and (perhaps) Fitzgerald, when every writer was summoned to the bar of style and the test of inwardness and self-consciousness, of the private life in general, where both Dreiser and Wright were found wanting.

Nothing so clearly dates Baldwin's early essays, especially the attacks on Wright, than the assurance that the novel has intrinsically little to do with society, but rather with "something more than that, something resolutely indefinable, unpredictable . . . the disquieting complexity of ourselves . . . this web of ambiguity, paradox, this hunger, danger, darkness . . . this power of revelation which is the business of the novelist, this journey toward a more vast reality which must take precedence over all other claims." I excerpt these phrases from "Everybody's Protest Novel," Baldwin's famous attack on *Uncle Tom's Cabin* and *Native Son,* which still seemed persuasive ten years ago but now, with its upper case mockery of "Causes" and a writer's "Responsibility," seems fatally marred by the end-of-ideology mood that produced it. It is a nice question how a purely formalist conception of the novel came to be articulated not so much through Jamesian notions of craft—though there was much of that—but through a pseudo-metaphysical rhetoric, a kitsch existentialism, bordering less on mysticism than on gibberish. Yet writers spoke of the novel that way all the time, as a mysterious inward quest, toward some ineffable region of personality. Mailer spoke of the novel that way, still does perhaps, and became the only one of the band to make something of such hash. What chance had Richard Wright in that climate of critical 'thinking'?

Native Son is an untidy novel, many novels. It looks backward to *An American Tragedy,* sideways to a lurid potboiler, forward, strikingly, to *L'Etranger* and the ideas of Sartre. Two-thirds of the way through it changes horses and devolves into a curious but inert ideological essay on a novel that has essentially ended, but that had until then been remarkably free of the clichés of proletarian fiction and the party line. This immensely long and disappointing coda has served to obscure the book and date it. The hidden strength of *Native Son*—hidden from formalist and Communist alike—is in essence Dostoevskyan rather than Mike Goldian: a harrowing mastery of extreme situations, of the mind *in extremis,* a medium not so much naturalistic as hallucinatory, dreamlike and poetic. Here are two sentences from a paragraph describing a man's hunger; Bigger Thomas is in flight, trapped, hungry, cold: "He wanted to pull off his clothes and roll in the snow until something nourishing seeped into his body through the pores of his skin. He wanted to grip something in his hands so hard it would turn to food." Psychologically this is vivid, almost surreal, but also it is socially emblematic, a fierce heightening of the whole condition of the ghetto where he is trapped, within a police cordon which only makes more literal the color line that divides it from the rest of the city.

To Wright hunger is not an absence of food but a form of violence. "Hunger came to his stomach," the same paragraph begins: "an icy hand reached down his throat and clutched his intestines and tied them into a cold, tight knot that ached." If this is less effective than the two later sentences it is because the violence of society is less palpable than the counter-violence that Bigger Thomas represents. In convicting society Wright thus slips toward luridness and cheap symbolism (as when Bigger is later "crucified" in the same white omnipresence of the snow), and finally, endless theorizing: Wright is forcing his theme. But in depicting Bigger from the inside and giving his fantasies and feelings a more-than-private shape, Wright truly approximates Lukács' description of classical realism as the union of the personal and the general, the fully rendered type, Hegel's concrete universal.

It was just this social dimension, which Dreiser and other American realists shared, that dropped out of serious American fiction toward the end of the forties. "Social affairs," Baldwin announced in the preface to his first book of essays, *Notes of a Native Son* (1955), "are not generally speaking the writer's prime concern, whether they ought to be or not." Baldwin's novels illustrate this lame conviction all too painfully. As Eldridge Cleaver said of *Another Country,* "his characters all seem to be fucking and sucking in a vacuum." On the other hand that same preface is titled "Autobiographical Notes," and we ought not to underestimate the boldness and healthy egotism of Baldwin's thrusting his private case forward as significant public example. Baldwin had before him, as he later acknowledged, the precedent of *Black Boy,* which itself sprang out of the autobiographical preface to *Uncle Tom's Children,* but there was little else to encourage him to break the then-prevalent mold of the impersonal artist who peers at the public through the coy mask of his "works"—a mold to which he generally adhered in his novels, as Mailer did. Later the precedent of Baldwin himself would make Mailer's own breakthrough more thinkable. *Advertisements for Myself,* with its rich, bloody life mostly in the italics of its autobiographical transitions, appeared four years after *Notes of a Native Son.* And *The Armies of the Night* is quite deliberately Mailer's *Fire Next Time,* the essay that would explode into a book, the journalistic occasion that transforms itself into a crucial act of self-definition.

But where Baldwin and even Mailer—despite his fascination with power—must *reach out* to their public subjects (the Black Muslims, the Pentagon march), then only to make that distance, that ambivalence, their true subjects, Wright's *Black Boy,* though more purely autobiographical, sits in effortless mastery over *its* social theme, the condition of the black man in the South. Yet Wright's book is also more convincingly personal, even in incidents he may have invented. Neither Baldwin nor Mailer, immense egos both, have as yet written true autobiographies; their revelations are obsessive but selective. Genuine sons of the forties and fifties, they remain essentially private persons despite their fame. Wright, however, a disaffected son of the thirties, did write an autobiography at age 37, but honed and sorted his memories into a coherent fable, aiming, like all great autobiographers, to fashion a myth rather than to convey information about the past.

In scene after scene Wright presents his younger self as a rebellious misfit, incapable of adapting to the modes of deference that obtain in his coarse and brutal family and in Southern life as a whole. On the very first page, as a four-year-old boy, he sets fire to the curtains, nearly incinerates his ailing grandmother, and almost ends his own life by taking refuge under the burning house. When his desperate parents finally rescue him, they show relief by beating him into unconsciousness, nearly killing him themselves. This pattern of instinctive rebellion and savage counter-violence recurs repeatedly though more subtly throughout the book. When he goes out at last among whites Wright makes an extreme effort of self-restraint, but try as he will there is always a touch of pride and self-respect, a touch of the uppity nigger about him. A latecomer to the white world, he is unable to quite master the shuffling, degraded, but apparently contented, manner that will tell whites he not only knows his place but loves it. He is the perennial loser, always half-willingly skirting an abyss, awaiting the fatal misstep that might reveal his true feelings and get him killed.

The turning point comes in an incident which reverses this pattern and shows him (and us) the true nature of his situation. He goes to work for a benevolent Yankee, but soon is typically hounded and threatened by two white co-workers. They warn him to leave the job. He wilts briefly, but returns the next day to see the boss, who quickly invites him to tell his story. It would seem that a great moment has come. For the first time a quantum of power is on his side. Instead, his sassiness and pride, irrepressible before, completely desert him. "An impulse to speak rose in me and died with the realization that I was facing a wall that I would never breech. . . . What would I accomplish by telling him? I was black; I lived in the South. . . . I looked at the white faces of Pease and Reynolds; I imagined their waylaying me, killing me. I remembered what had happened to Ned's brother."

The writer, with characteristic economy, does not belabor the lesson of this most humiliating of all moments, but to the reader it is clear enough: there can be no separate peace, no private accommodation. Neither the well-meaning Yankee, archetype of the ineffectual liberal paternalist, nor the defeated but unbroken black boy can buck the whole Southern way of life. Wright will break the mold by escaping to the North, becoming a writer and radical who will turn his rebelliousness from an ineluctable fatality to a fighting virtue. With word and deed he will try to change society rather than nest in the shelter of its exceptions.

Wright's books, especially *Black Boy,* enunciate a fundamental pattern of black writing, that of the *Bildungsroman,* or, How I got my consciousness raised. The black writer is almost by definition someone who has made it, struggled out of the cave not only of oppression but illusion — a mental bondage that issues in impotence and self-hatred—and has come to deliver an account of his journey. Thus *Native Son* moves from a crime-and-punishment plot to the story of how Bigger Thomas, by accepting his crime, achieves a measure of freedom and awareness—"what I killed for, I am." But the theme and its material increasingly clash; the crime is finally *not* acceptable, nor reducible to symbolism. Pursuing the matter, Wright's own liberated consciousness becomes too heavy, too subtle for Bigger, yet remains too entangled in the remnants of the murder plot to evade moral confusion.

Ralph Ellison complains that "Bigger Thomas had none of the finer qualities of Richard Wright, none of the imagination, none of the sense of poetry, none of the gaiety," and in his own novel, *Invisible Man,* he transposed the *Bildungsroman* into a freewheeling and episodic form whose hero could brook diverse kinds of consciousness. In prose black writers generally tend toward an urgent but impure mixture of fiction, autobiography and discursiveness, and the most original thing about *Invisible Man* is its eclecticism and discontinuity, akin to the black humorists of the sixties, where technical and verbal inventiveness fills the place of realistic setting and psychology. Yet Ellison's book essentially follows the pattern of *Black Boy* and *Native Son,* as do Malcolm's autobiography, *Soul on Ice, Soledad Brother,* and George Cain's recent, very impressive novel *Blueschild Baby,* whose hero is named George Cain, where the distinction between fiction and autobiography has disappeared entirely. In this last book only the scene and subject change, not the basic pattern: for Cain the journey goes not from South to North but from heroin-addiction, prison, and self-hatred to self-respect, to writing, and above all, as with Cleaver, back to the arms of the black woman. Even more classically, Malcolm's autobiography re-enacts the fundamental pattern of spiritual autobiography since Augustine, built around not one but two deep conversions—first to the Nation of Islam, then from black racism to a brand of humane radicalism that might have made him one of the crucial American leaders. (Malcolm even parallels Augustine in richly conveying the pleasures of the unconverted life.)

James Baldwin is a distinctive figure here, with his spiritual style rooted in the Negro church, but his essays follow the pattern far more than his novels do, and this helps account for their superiority. Baldwin's problem as a novelist is not simply his difficulty in fully imagining other people, or his inability to take the form in hand, as Ellison did, and mold it to his own vision. (Ellison himself, accepting the National Book Award, aptly stressed the importance of the novel's "experimental attitude.") It has been Baldwin's misfortune to move from one false notion of the novel—the New Critical one, that of a highly crafted, distanced object—to the exact opposite fallacy, by which an aimless assortment of characters serve as threadbare masks for a purely personal set of obsessions and intensities. If *Another Country* is shapeless at least the feelings are still vigorous and sharp, but by the last novel, a long, dismal failure called *Tell Me How Long the Train's Been Gone* (1968), Baldwin the novelist seems to have lost all ability to command belief. If anything he is more rather than less obsessed by the formative incidents of his childhood, but they have become more distant and abstract even as they have extended their hold on him; and to dramatize the later experiences of fame and success he can bring no spirit at all. (These impressions are bolstered by *A Rap on Race,* his recent book of conversations with Margaret Mead, a typical publisher's brainchild.)

By all accounts Baldwin's life has been much entwined with white people and white books; he deeply resisted having his consciousness raised in the direction of separatism; *The Fire Next Time* summarizes his ambivalence even as it burns with the intensity of his anger. Now he is nowhere, an expatriate again, *all* anger—though the lengthening chain of corpses from Malcolm to George Jackson does much to make his feelings plausible. It is ironic that the man who is partly responsible for the current black mood, should also fall victim to it. Baldwin's later essays become very harsh, and powerfully anticipate the anti-integratist militance that developed in the mid-sixties. "Do I really *want* to be integrated into a burning house?," he asked in *The Fire Next Time.* Earlier, in 1961, he summed up his message by saying that "to be a Negro in this country and to be relatively conscious, is to be in a rage all the time."

But for Baldwin that rage was a torment and an anguish; he quickly added that "the first problem is how to control that rage so it won't destroy you." For the angry young blacks of the sixties, who perhaps avoided the worst scars that Baldwin and Wright received so early, rage is their pride and power, not a poison at the wellspring. Thus the paradox that while Baldwin has rehashed and flattened what was once a richly complicated, ironic view of the race problem in America, partly out of a desperate attempt to keep abreast of the new mood, younger black writers regularly define their own positions by attacking him, much as he once attacked Richard Wright.

A Bibliography of Richard Wright's Works

MICHEL FABRE AND EDWARD MARGOLIES

This chronological bibliography of Wright's published works (to the exclusion of interviews, transcripts of public pronouncements and collective appeals whose authorship is uncertain) is a revised and enlarged version of the one which originally appeared in *Bulletin of Bibliography* (Jan. 1965) and which was reprinted at the end of Constance Webb's *Richard Wright* (1969) and in the Jan. 1969 issue of *Negro Digest.* I have corrected a few errors, reorganized the headings, added some twenty short, but at times important, items and provided comments and dates of composition (between brackets) when differing from year of publication. As a rule, only first appearances are indicated, reprints being given only when in book form or significantly different. When first published in translation abroad, an item is indicated under first U.S. publication, unless it has never been published in English.

This bibliography will be part of a book-size, annotated international bibliography of the published and unpublished writings, interviews, broadcasts, etc. by and about Richard Wright.

Michel Fabre

A. POETRY:

"A Red Love Note," *Left Front,* no. 3 (Jan.-Feb. 1934), 3. [1933]

"Rest for the Weary," *Left Front,* no. 3 (Jan.-Feb. 1934), 3. [1933]

"Strength," *The Anvil,* no. 5 (March-April 1934), 20. [1933]

"Child of the Dead and Forgotten Gods," *The Anvil,* no. 5 (March-April 1934), 30. [1933]

"Everywhere Burning Waters Rise," *Left Front,* no. 4 (May-June 1934), 9.

"I Have Seen Black Hands," *New Masses,* 11 (June 26, 1934), 16. [1933]

"Obsession," *Midland Left,* no. 2 (Feb. 1935), 14.

"Live and Rise," *Midland Left,* no. 2 (Feb. 1935), 13-14.

"I Am a Red Slogan," *International Literature,* 4 (April 1935), 35. [1934]

"Ah Feels It in Mah Bones," *International Literature,* 4 (April 1935) 80 [1934]

"Red Leaves of Red Books," *New Masses,* 15 (April 30, 1935), 6.

"Between the World and Me," *Partisan Review,* 2 (July-August 1935), 18-19. [1934]

"Spread Your Sunrise," *New Masses,* 16 (July 2, 1935), 26. [1934]

"Transcontinental," *International Literature,* 1 (Jan. 1936), 52-57. [1935]

"Hearst Headline Blues," *New Masses,* 19 (May 12, 1936), 14.

"Old Habit and New Love," *New Masses,* 21 (Dec. 15, 1936), 29.

"We of the Streets," *New Masses,* 23 (April 13, 1937), 14. [1936]

"Red Clay Blues," *New Masses,* 32 (Aug. 1, 1939), 14. Written in collaboration with Langston Hughes.

"King Joe" ("Joe Louis Blues"), lyrics for OKEH Record no. 6475. Reprinted in *New York Amsterdam Star News,* Oct. 18, 1941, p. c 16. [Oct. 3, 1941]

"Haiku Poems." A number of haikus have appeared successively in Ollie Harrington, "The Last Days of Richard Wright," *Ebony,* 16 (Feb. 1961), 93-94. Reprinted in Arna Bontemps and Langston Hughes, *The Poetry of the Negro,* 1964 edition. [8 poems] (2) Constance Webb, *Richard Wright: a Biography,* New York, Putnam, 1968, p. 393-94. [4 poems] (3) Richard Wright, "Haikus," *Studies in Black Literature,* I (Autumn 1970), 3, followed by a study of Richard Wright's poetry by Michel Fabre.

B. FICTION:

"[The Voodoo of] Hell's Half Acre," *Southern Register* (Jackson, Miss.), circa spring 1924. No complete version available. [1924]

"Superstition," *Abbot's Monthly Magazine,* 2 (April 1931), 45-47, 64-66, 72-73. Signed Richard N. Wright. [1930]

"Big Boy Leaves Home," in *The New Caravan* (eds. Alfred Kreymborg et al., New York, 1936), 124-158. Included in *Uncle Tom's Children.* [1935]

"Silt," *New Masses,* 24 (August 24, 1937), 19-20. Included in *Eight Men* as "The Man Who Saw the Flood." [1936-37]

"Fire and Cloud," *Story Magazine,* 12 (March 1938), 9-41. Included in *Uncle Tom's Children.* Was awarded the Story Magazine Prize in Dec. 1937. [1936]

Uncle Tom's Children: four novellas. Harper, New York, 1938, 317 p. Includes "Big Boy Leaves Home," "Down by the Riverside," [1936] "Long Black Song," [1936] and "Fire and Cloud."

"Bright and Morning Star," *New Masses,* 27 (May 10, 1938), 97-99, 116-124. Included in *Uncle Tom's Children* (1940 edition) and published in booklet form by International Publishers in 1941. [1937]

"Almos' A Man," *Harper's Bazaar,* 74 (Jan. 1940), 40-41. Included, with slight revisions, in *Eight Men* as "The Man Who Was Almost a Man." Revised version of last two chapters of unpublished novel, "Tarbaby's Dawn." [1934-37]

Native Son. New York, Harper, 1940, 359 p. [1937-39]

Uncle Tom's Children: five long stories. New York, Harper, 1940, 384 p. Includes "The Ethics of Living Jim Crow," the short stories printed in the 1938 edition and "Bright and Morning Star."

Native Son, the Biography of a Young American. A Play in Ten Scenes. By Paul Green and Richard Wright. New York, Harper, 1941, 148 p. In spite of Paul Green's recent claims, Wright's collaboration in the actual writing of the stage adaptation was important. [1940-41]

"The Man Who Lived Underground," *Accent,* 2 (Spring 1942), 170-176. Excerpts from a novel, differs distinctly from the novella printed in *Cross Section.* 1944. [1941]

"The Man Who Lived Underground," *Cross Section* (ed. Edwin Seaver, New York, 1944), 58-102. Included in *Eight Men.* Second part of a novel, the first part of which is unpublished. [1941]

"The Man Who Killed a Shadow," *Zero* (Paris), I (Spring 1949), 45-53. First published as "L'homme qui tua une ombre," *Les Lettres Françaises,* 4 Oct. 1946, p. 1, 10. Included in *Eight Men.* [1945-46]

The Outsider. New York, Harper, 1953, 405 p. [1947-52]

Savage Holiday. New York, Avon, 1954, 220 p. [1953]

"Big Black Good Man," *Esquire,* 50 (Nov. 1957), 76-80. Included in *Eight Men.* [1956]

The Long Dream. New York, Doubleday, 1958, 384 p. [1956-57]

Eight Men. Cleveland and New York, World Publishing Company, 1961, 250 p. Includes "The Man Who Went to Chicago," "The Man Who Saw the Flood," "The Man Who Was Almost a Man," "Big, Black Good Man," "Man, God Ain't Like That," "Man of All Works," "The Man Who Lived Underground," "The Man Who Killed a Shadow." [Collection prepared by Wright in 1960]

Lawd Today. New York, Walker, 1963, 189 p. [1931-37; published posthumously]

"Five Episodes" in *Soon, One Morning* (ed. Herbert Hill, New York, 1963), 140-64. Excerpts from "Island of Hallucinations," an unpublished novel completed in 1959.

C. NON-FICTION:

1. Books:

12 Million Black Voices: A Folk History of the Negro in the United States. Photo direction by Edwin Rosskam. New York, Viking Press, 1941, 152 p.

Black Boy: A Record of Childhood and Youth. New York, Harper, 1945, 258 p. [1942-43] Represents first section of unpublished "American Hunger" volume. Includes "The Ethics of Living Jim Crow."

Black Power: A Record of Reactions in a Land of Pathos. New York, Harper, 1954, 358 p. [1953-54] From the diary of a visit to the Gold Coast. Includes "What Is Africa to Me?"

The Color Curtain. Cleveland and New York, World Publishing Company, 1956, 221 p. [1955] First published as *Bandoeng, 1.500.000.000 hommes.* Paris, Calman-Lévy, 1955, 203 p. (trans. Hélène Claireau). Includes "Vers Bandoeng Via Séville," "Le Congrès des hommes de couleur," "Indonesian Notebook," and "Le monde occidental à Bandoeng."

Pagan Spain. New York, Harper, 1956, 241 p. [1954-56]

White Man, Listen. New York, Doubleday, 1957, 190 p. Includes a slightly revised version of "Littérature noire américaine," "Tradition and Industrialization, the Plight of the Tragic Elite in Africa" and other previously unpublished essays and lectures.

2. Articles, essays, lectures, etc.:

"The Ethics of Living Jim Crow, an Autobiographical Sketch," in *American Stuff* (W.P.A. Writers' anthology), New York, 1937, p. 39-52. Included in *Uncle Tom's Children* (1940 edition). Incorporated in *Black Boy.* [1936]

"Portrait of Harlem," in *New York Panorama* (ed. New York W.P.A.), New York, 1938, p. 132-51. Unsigned. [1937]

"Blueprint for Negro Writing," *New Challenge,* II (Fall 1937), 53-65. The text published in *Amistad II* (1970) is, in fact, an earlier version of this essay which Wright himself edited and rearranged in August 1937, and it should not be regarded as the final one.

"How 'Uncle Tom's Children' Grew," *Columbia University Writers' Club Bulletin,* II (May 1938). [p. 16-18]

"Can We Depend upon Youth to Follow the American Way?" *Town Meeting Bulletin,* 4 (April 24, 1939), 15-17. Participation in panel discussion.

"How 'Bigger' Was Born," *Saturday Review,* 22 (June 1, 1940), 4-5, 17-20. Nearly complete version of a March 1940 lecture later published in pamphlet form *(Harper,* 1940, 39 p.).

"I Bite the Hand that Feeds Me," *Atlantic Monthly,* 155 (June 1940), 826-28. Reply to a review of *Native Son* by David L. Cohn in the May 1940 issue of *Atlantic Monthly.*

"Rascoe Baiting," *American Mercury,* 50 (July 1940), 376-77. Reply to a review of *Native Son* by Burton Rascoe in the May 1940 issue of *American Mercury.*

"Statement in Support of Browder and Ford," *Daily Worker,* Sept. 30, 1940, p. 15.

"What Do I Think of the Theater?" *New York World-Telegram,* March 2, 1941, p. 20. On the stage adaptation of *Native Son.*

"Not My Peoples' War," *New Masses,* 39 (June 17, 1941), 8-9, 12.

"U.S. Negroes Greet You," *Daily Worker,* Sept. 1, 1941, p. 4. Reprinted as "I Support the Soviet Union" in *Soviet Russia Today,* Sept. 1941, p. 29. [A cable sent to *International Literature* following the Nazi attack]

"What You Don't Know Won't Hurt You," *Harper's Magazine,* 186 (Dec. 1942), 58-61. Partly fictionalized Chicago memories later incorporated into the manuscript of "American Hunger."

"Twelve Million Black Voices," *Coronet,* 15 (April 1942), 23-93. Introduction, extracts of *Twelve Million Black Voices* and verse captions for photographs from the book.

"The Negro and Parkway Community House," Chicago, 1943, 4 p. Pamphlet written at the request of Horace Cayton, director of this Chicago institution in April 1941.

"I Tried to Be a Communist," *Atlantic Monthly,* 159 (Aug. 1944), 61-70; (Sept. 1944), 48-56. Part of the second section of "American Hunger," the original manuscript of *Black Boy.* Later included in *The God that Failed* (ed. Richard Crossman, New York, 1949). [1942-43]

"Richard Wright Describes the Birth of *Black Boy,*" *New York Post,* Nov. 30, 1944, p. B6.

"Early Days in Chicago," in *Cross Section* (ed. Edwin Seaver, New York, 1945), 306-342. Included in *Eight Men.* Part of second section of "American Hunger" manuscript. [1942-43]

"Is America Solving Its Race Problem?" *America's Town Meeting of the Air Bulletin,* 11 (May 24, 1945), 6-7. Participation in panel discussion.

"American Hunger," *Mademoiselle,* 21 (Sept. 1945), 164-65, 299-301. This is only part of the second manuscript section of "American Hunger" which was left out of *Black Boy.* [1942-43]

"A hitherto unpublished manuscript by Richard Wright being a continuation of *Black Boy.*" Photo-offset pamphlet edited by Constance Webb for private circulation in July 1946. n.p. In spite of the title, only half a dozen pages from the second section of the "American Hunger" manuscript were unpublished at the time.

"A Paris les G.I. Noirs ont appris à connaître et à aimer la liberté," *Samedi Soir,* 25 mai 1946, p. 2.

"Psychiatry Comes to Harlem," *Free World,* 12 (Sept. 1946), 49-51. Reprinted as "Psychiatry Goes to Harlem" in *Twice a Year,* no. 14-15 (1946-47), 349-54. On the founding of the Lafargue Clinic.

"How Jim Crow Feels," *True Magazine,* (Nov. 1946), 25-27, 154-56. First published as "Je sais reconnaître un nègre du Sud . . . ," *Paris Matin,* 27 juin 1946, p. 2. On Wright's trip to Mexico and the South in the summer of 1940.

"A World View of the American Negro," *Twice A Year,* no. 14-15 (Fall 1946-Winter 1947), 346-48. First published as "Lettre sur le problème noir aux U.S.A." in *Les Nouvelles Epitres,* Paris, 1947, lettre 32 (with facsimile reproduction of July 1, 1946 letter).

"Urban Misery in an American City: Juvenile Delinquency in Harlem," *Twice A Year,* no. 14-15 (Fall 1946-Winter 1947), 339-45. [1945-46]

"Niam N'goura or *Présence Africaine's* Raison d'Etre," *Presence Africaine,* no. 1 (nov.-déc. 1947), 184-92. This is an adaptation, done in collaboration with Thomas Diop, of Alioune Diop's article in the same issue, 7-14.

"Littérature Noire Américaine," *Temps Modernes,* no. 35 (août 1948), 193-220. Included in *White Man, Listen.* [1944] This is the text of a lecture often given by Wright in 1945 in the U.S.

"L'humanité est plus grande que l'Amérique ou la Russie," *Franc-Tireur* (Paris), 16 déc. 1948, p. 4. Speech given at a "Rassemblement Démocratique Révolutionnaire" congress in Paris on Dec. 10, 1948.

"L'homme du Sud," *France Etats-Unis,* Dec. 1950, p. 2. On William Faulkner.

"Richard Wright Explains Ideas about Movie Making," *Ebony,* 6 (Jan. 1951), 84-85. On the shooting of "Native Son" in Argentina. [1950]

"American Negroes in France," *The Crisis,* 58 (June-July 1951), 381-83. First published as "Les Noirs Américains et la France" in *France-Observateur,* no. 56 (3 mai 1951).

"Derrière l'affaire [McGee]," *Le Droit de Vivre* (Paris), 15 mai 1951, 1. On the trial and execution of Willie McGee.

"The Shame of Chicago," *Ebony,* 7 (Dec. 1951), 24-32. On Wright's return to Chicago in 1949. [1950]

"There is Always Another Cafe," *The Kiosk* (Paris), no. 10, 1953, p. 12-14.

"What Is Africa to Me?" *Encounter,* 3 (Sept. 1954), 22-31. Included in *Black Power.* [1953]

"Deux portraits africains," *Preuves,* no. 45 (Nov. 1954), 3-6. From the first unpublished chapter of the manuscript of *Black Power.* [1953]

"Vers Bandoeng via Séville," *Preuves,* no. 53 (juillet 1955), 6-9. Incorporated in *The Color Curtain.*

"Le congrès des hommes de couleur," Preuves, no. 54 (août 1955), 42-48. Incorporated in *The Color Curtain.*

"Indonesian Notebook," *Encounter,* 5 (August 1955), 24-31. Incorporated in *The Color Curtain.*

"Le monde occidental à Bandoeng," *Preuves,* no. 55 (sept. 1955), 45-55. Incorporated in *The Color Curtain.*

"Tradition and Industrialization: the Plight of the Tragic Elite in Africa," *Présence Africaine,* no. 8-10 (juin-nov. 1956), 347-60. Included in *White Man, Listen.* Paper given at the First Congress of Black Artists and Intellectuals in Paris, Sept. 1956.

"De la Côte de l'Or au Ghana," *Preuves,* no. 75 (mai 1957), 11-14.

"Le Noir est une création du Blanc," *Preuves,* no. 87 (mai 1958), 40-41. Answer to a list of questions on Black culture.

"Spanish Snapshots: Granada, Seville," *Two Cities,* no. 2 (July 1959), 25-34. Part of the unpublished section of the *Pagan Spain* manuscript. [1954-55]

"Espagne Payenne," *Haute Société,* no. 3 (nov. 1960), 34-38. On Spanish festivals.

"Harlem," *Les Parisiens,* no. 1 (déc. 1960), 23

"Le jazz et le désir," *Les Cahiers du Jazz,* no. 4 (printemps 1961), 53-54.

3. Book Reviews and comments on books:

"A Tale of Folk Courage," *Partisan Review and Anvil,* 3 (April 1936), 31. Review of *Black Thunder* by Arna Bontemps.

"Between Laughter and Tears," *New Masses,* 25 (Oct. 5, 1937), 22-25. Review of *These Low Grounds* by Waters E. Turpin and *Their Eyes Were Watching God* by Zora Neale Hurston.

"A Sharecropper's Story," *New Republic,* 93 (Dec. 1, 1937), 109. Review of *I Was a Sharecropper* by Harry B. Kroll.

"Adventure and Love in Loyalist Spain," *New Masses,* 26 (March 8, 1938), 25-26. Review of *The Wall of Men* by William Rollins.

"Lynching Bee," *New Republic,* 102 (March 11, 1940), 351. Review of *Trouble in July* by Erskine Caldwell.

"Richard Wright Reviews James Weldon Johnson's Classic 'Black Manhattan'," *Chicago News,* May 22, 1940, p. 10.

"Inner Landscape," *New Republic,* 103 (Aug. 5, 1940), 195. Review of *The Heart Is a Lonely Hunter* by Carson McCullers.

"Forerunner and Ambassador," *New Republic,* 103 (Oct. 24, 1940), 600. Review of *The Big Sea* by Langston Hughes.

"As Richard Wright Sees Autobiographies of Langston Hughes and W.E.B. DuBois," *Chicago News,* Dec. 4, 1940, p. 10. Review of *The Big Sea* by Langston Hughes and *Dusk of Dawn* by W.E.B. DuBois.

Comment on *Let My People Go* by Henrietta Buckmaster, New York, Harper, 1941. On dust jacket.

"Gertrude Stein's Story Is Drenched in Hitler's Horrors," *P.M. Magazine,* March 11, 1945, p. m 15. Review of *Wars I Have Seen* by Gertrude Stein.

"A Non-Combat Soldier Strips Words for Action," *P.M. Magazine,* June 24, 1945, p. m 16. Review of *The Brick Foxhole* by Richard Brooks.

"Alger Revisited, or My Stars! Did We Read That Stuff?" *P.M. Magazine,* Sept. 16, 1945, p. m 8. Review of Horatio Alger's *Collected Novels.*

"Two Novels of the Crushing of Men, One White, One Black," *P.M. Magazine,* Nov. 25, 1945, p. m 7- m 8. Review of *Focus* by Arthur Miller and *If He Hollers Let Him Go* by Chester Himes.

Comment on Dorsha Hayes, *Who Walks with the Earth,* New York, 1945. Back dust jacket.

Comment on Marianne Oswald's *One Small Voice,* New York, 1946. Back dust jacket.

"*Wasteland* Uses Psychoanalysis Deftly," *P.M. Magazine,* Feb. 17, 1946, p. m 8. Review of *Wasteland* by Jo Sinclair (pseud. for Ruth Seid).

"A Steinian Catechism," back dust jacket of Gertrude Stein's *Brewsie and Willie,* New York, 1946. [April 1946]

"American G.I.'s Fears Worry Gertrude Stein," *P.M. Magazine,* July 26, 1946, p. m 15- m 16. Review of *Brewsie and Willie* by Gertrude Stein in the form of a letter to Roger Pipett.

"E. M. Forster Anatomizes the Novel," *P.M. Magazine,* March 16, 1947, p. m 3. Review of *Aspects of the Novel* by E. M. Forster.

"A Junker's Epic Novel on Militarism," *P.M. Magazine,* May 4, 1947, p. m 3. Review of *The End Is Not Yet* by Fritz Von Unruh.

[Comment on] *A Street in Bronzeville,* by Gwendolyn Brooks, on back dust jacket of *Annie Allen,* by Gwendolyn Brooks (Harper, 1949).

Comment on Jean Genet, *Our Lady of the Flowers,* New York, 1950. Back dust jacket. Written at the request of Bernard Frechtman in 1949.

"Neurosis of Conquest," *The Nation,* 183 (Oct. 20, 1956), 330-31. Review of *Prospero and Caliban* by Octave Mannoni.

"The Voiceless Ones," *Saturday Review,* 43 (April 16, 1960), 53-54. Review of *The Disinherited* by Michel Del Castillo.

4. Prefaces, introductions, forewords, etc.:

"Foreword," *Illinois Labor Notes,* 4 (March 1936), 2. Foreword to the special issue devoted to the first National Negro Congress meeting in Chicago.

"Richard Wright," in *The New Caravan,* ed. Alfred Kreymborg et al., New York, 1936, p. 663. Short biographical notice.

"Introduction," in Howard Nutt, *Special Laughter*, Prairie City, Illinois, Press of James Decker, 1940, ix-xii. In the form of a letter, dated Spring 1940.

Note on Theodore Ward, pamphlet for the *Negro Playwright's Company,* New York, 1940, p. 3.

"Letter to International Publishers," in *Bright and Morning Star,* New York, International Publishers, 1941, 1. Is an introduction to the short story published as a booklet.

"Note on Jim Crow Blues," preface to Keynote Album no. 107, *Southern Exposure* (1941). Reprinted as "Note sur les Blues" in *La Revue du Jazz,* avril 1949, 113. [1941]

Prefatory note, Playbill for *Native Son,* St. James's Theatre, New York, March 1941, p. 1.

"Foreword," in Morris V. Schappes, *Letters from the Tombs,* New York, Schappes Defense Committee, 1941, v-vi.

[Why I Selected 'How Bigger Was Born'], in *This Is My Best,* ed. Whit Burnett, Philadelphia, 1942, p. 448. [July, 1942]

"Introduction," in Nelson Algren, *Never Come Morning,* New York, 1942, ix-x.

"Introduction," in Jay Saunders Redding, *No Day of Triumph,* New York, Harper, 1942, 1.

"Don't Wear Your Sunday Best Every Day," 140-word advertisement for War Bonds on back of dust jacket of *Black Boy* (1945).

"Introduction," in Horace R. Cayton and St. Clair Drake, *Black Metropolis,* New York, Harcourt-Brace, 1945, xvii-xxxiv.

"Why I Chose 'Melanctha' by Gertrude Stein," in *I Wish I'd Written That,* ed. Whit Burnett, New York, 1946, p. 234.

"Evidence de l'Art Nègre," introduction to a pamphlet for an African art exhibition at Librairie Palmes, Paris, p. 1. [Nov. 1948]

"Richard Wright présente le Musée Vivant," *Le Musée Vivant,* 12 (nov. 1948), p. 1. Introduction to a special issue on Negro art.

"Preface" to "Human, All Too Human" by E. Franklin Frazier, *Présence Africaine,* no. 6 (janvier-mars 1949), 47.

"Introducing Some American Negro Folk Songs," *Présence Africaine,* no. 6 (janvier-mars 1949), 70.

"Introductory Note to 'The Respectful Prostitute' [by Jean-Paul Sartre]," in *Art and Action, a Book of Literature, the Arts and Civil Liberties, (Twice a Year* Tenth Anniversary Issue) New York, 1948, 14-16.

"Introduction to 'American Hunger'," in *The World's Best,* ed. Whit Burnett, New York, 1950, p. 303. First published as "Richard Wright nous présente *Black Boy*" in *L'Ordre* (Paris), 14 janvier 1948, p. 3.

"Preface," in Chester Himes, *La Croisade de Lee Gordon,* Paris, Corréa, 1952, 7-8. Himes's *Lonely Crusade* was published in the U.S. without a preface.

"Introduction," in George Lamming, *In the Castle of my Skin,* New York, 1953, ix-xii.

"Introduction," in George Padmore, *Pan-Africanism or Communism?,* London, Dobson, 1956, 11-14. Translated and revised as a preface to *Panafricanisme ou Communisme,* Paris, *Présence Africaine,* 1960, 9-12. [March 2, 1956 and Sept. 10, 1960]

"Une pièce qui aurait ravi Voltaire," L'Avant-Scène, no. 168 (1958), 3-4. Introduction to Louis Sapin's *Papa Bon Dieu,* which Wright adapted as *Daddy Goodness* the same year.

"Au lecteur français," in *Ecoute, Homme Blanc,* Paris, Calman-Lévy, 1959, xv-xxxvi. Special foreword for the French reader, dated 1959, to accompany the translation of *White Man, Listen* by Dominque Guillet.

"Foreword," in Paul Oliver, *Blues Fell This Morning,* London, Horizon Press, 1960, vii-xii.

["The Past is Still with Us"], introduction to "Les Rois du Caf'Conç," Barclay Album 80 128. [1960]

["So Long, Big Bill Broonzy"], introduction to "The Blues of Big Bill Broonzy," Mercury Album 7198 Standard. [1960, unsigned]

"Introduction," in Françoise Gourdon, *Tant qu'il y aura la peur,* Paris, Flammarion, 1961, 1-3.

5. Newspaper reporting and journalism:

"Joe Louis Uncovers Dynamite," *New Masses,* 17 (Oct. 8, 1935), 18.

"Two Million Black Voices," *New Masses,* 18 (Feb. 25, 1936), 16.

"Negro Writers Launch Literary Quarterly," *Daily Worker,* June 8, 1937, p. 7. On *New Challenge.*

"Young Writers Launch Literary Quarterly," *San Antonio Register,* July 10, 1937, p. 4. On *New Challenge.*

"Protests against Slugging Grow, Butcher Who Attacked Negro Boy Is Fired," *Daily Worker,* July 15, 1937, p. 3.

"Negro, with 3-Week Old Baby, Begs Food on Streets," *Daily Worker,* August 4, 1937, p. 3.

"C P Leads Struggle for Freedom, Stachel Says," *Daily Worker,* August 9, 1937, p. 2.

"Huddie Ledbetter, Famous Negro Folk Artist," *Daily Worker,* August 12, 1937, p. 7.

"Communist Leader Warns on Harlem Tiger Stooges," *Daily Worker,* August 13, 1937, p. 4.

"What Happens in a C P Branch Party Meeting in the Harlem Section," *Daily Worker,* August 16, 1937, p. 6.

"Pullman Porters to Celebrate 12th Year of Their Union," *Daily Worker,* August 19, 1937, p. 3.

"Scottsboro Boys on Stage is Opposed," *Daily Worker,* August 21, 1937, p. 3.

"Born a Slave, She Recruits 5 Members for Communist Party," *Daily Worker,* August 30, 1937, p. 2.

"Harlem Women Hit Boost on Milk Price," *Daily Worker,* Sept. 3, 1937, p. 3.

"Insect Ridden Medicine Given in Hospital," *Daily Worker,* Sept. 4, 1937, p. 5.

"Mrs. Holmes and Daughter Drink from the Fountain of Communism," *Daily Worker,* Sept. 7, 1937, p. 5.

"'Horseplay' at Lafayette Fun for Children and Grownups Alike," *Daily Worker,* Sept. 11, 1937, p. 7.

"Harlem Spanish Women Come out of the Kitchen," *Daily Worker,* Sept. 20, 1937, p. 5.

"10,000 Negro Vets in New York Silent, but They're Talking Up at Home," *Daily Worker,* Sept. 23, 1937, p. 4.

"Big Harlem Rally for China Tonight," *Daily Worker,* Sept. 27, 1937, p. 4.

"2 American Negroes in Key Posts of Spain's Loyalist Forces," *Daily Worker,* Sept. 29, 1937, p. 2.

"Randolph Urges Parley between AFL-CIO Unions," *Daily Worker,* Sept. 30, 1937, p. 3.

"Bates Tells of Spain's Fight for Strong Republican Army," *Daily Worker,* Oct. 1, 1937, p. 2.

"Negro Youth on March, Says Leader," *Daily Worker,* Oct. 7, 1937, p. 3.

"Opening on Harlem Project Homes Show How Slums Can be Wiped Out in New York," *Daily Worker,* Oct. 8, 1937, p. 5.

"See Biggest Negro Parley since Days of Reconstruction," *Daily Worker,* Oct. 14, 1937, p. 5.

"Negro Tradition in the Theatre," *Daily Worker,* Oct. or Nov. 15, 1937, p. 5.

"Harlem, Bronx Sign Competition Pact," *Daily Worker,* Oct. 19, 1937, p. 5.

"Harlem Negro Leaders Back Mayor for Liberal Views," *Daily Worker,* Oct. 20, 1937, p. 5.

"Browder Warns of Growth of Fascism in Latin America," *Daily Worker,* Oct. 23, 1937, p. 5.

"New Negro Pamphlet Stresses Need for U.S. People's Front," *Daily Worker,* Oct. 25, 1937, p. 2.

"Harlem Leaders Rap *Amsterdam News,* Stand for Mahoney," *Daily Worker,* Oct. 30, 1937, p. 6.

"Harlem Vote Swings Away from Tiger," *Daily Worker,* Nov. 2, 1937, p. 3.

"Negro Leaders Hail Victory of ALP at New York Polls," *Daily Worker,* Nov. 4, 1937, p. 5.

"ALP Assemblyman Urges State Control," *Daily Worker,* Nov. 8, 1937, p. 1.

"Negro Social Worker Hails Housing, Education in Spain," *Daily Worker,* Nov. 12, 1937, p. 2.

"ALP Assemblyman in Harlem Hails Unity of Labor at Polls," *Daily Worker,* Nov. 18, 1937, p. 2.

"Walter Garland Tells What Spain's Fight Against Fascism Means to the Negro People," *Daily Worker,* Nov. 29, 1937, p. 2.

"'He Died by Them,' Hero's Widow Tells of Rescue of Negro Children," *Daily Worker,* Dec. 6, 1937, p. 1, 6.

"Harlem East Side Honor Hero Who Died in Rescue of Negroes," *Daily Worker,* Dec. 7, 1937, p. 4.

"Ban on Negro Doctors Bared at City Probe," *Daily Worker,* Dec. 15, 1937, p. 1.

"Gouging Landlord Discrimination against Negroes Bared at Hearing," *Daily Worker,* Dec. 15, 1937, p. 6.

"James W. Ford Celebrates 44th Birthday," *Daily Worker,* Dec. 23, 1937, p. 4.

"Santa Claus Has a Hard Time Finding Way in Harlem Slums," *Daily Worker,* Dec. 27, 1937, p. 4.

"Every Child Is a Genius," *Daily Worker,* Dec. 28, 1937, p. 7.

"Why the Eyes of the People Turn to the Ring for the Title Bout at Yankee Stadium Tonight," *Daily Worker,* June 22, 1938, p. 1, 4. On forthcoming Louis-Schmeling fight.

"How He Did It, and Oh!—Where Were Hitler's Pagan Gods?" *Daily Worker,* June 24, 1938, p. 1, 8. On Joe Louis's victory over Schmeling.

"High Tide in Harlem," *New Masses,* 28 (July 5, 1938), 18-20. On Louis's victory over Schmeling.

6. Correspondence:

"Letter to the Editors," *Partisan Review and Anvil,* 3 (June 1936), 30. In defense of progressive writer Meyer Levin, labelled a reactionary in an article published by the magazine.

"Reader's Right: Writers Ask Break for Negroes," New York *Post,* April 5, 1938, p. 20. Letter to the Editors.

"A Letter about the War in Spain," in *Writers Take Sides,* New York, League of American Writers, May 1938.

"Letter to Bruce Kaputska," *The Kaputskan,* 1 (Fall 1940), 17. [August 1940]

"Greetings," *New Masses,* 39 (Feb. 18, 1941), 14. Extract of a letter encouraging the magazine.

"To Sender Garlin," *Daily Worker,* Feb. 13, 1942, p. 7. Letter dated Feb. 10, 1942, asking for more consideration for readers' opinions.

"From Richard Wright," in *The Flowers of Friendship* (ed. Donald Gallup, New York, 1953), 379-80. Letter to Gertrude Stein dated May 27, 1945.

"Richard Wright and Antonio Frasconi: an Exchange of Letters," *Twice a Year,* no. 12-13 (1945), 256-61. [Nov. 1944]

"Two Letters to Dorothy Norman," in *Art and Action,* New York, 1948, 65-73. Includes a letter dated February 28, 1948 (p. 65-71) and a letter dated March 9, 1948 (p. 72-73) both from Paris, on the state of things in France and Europe.

"Comrade Strong, Don't You Remember?" New York *Herald Tribune* (European edition), April 4, 1949, p. 3. Letter to Anna Louise Strong in response to her article in the same newspaper.

"To Axel Lonnquist," New York *Herald Tribune* (European edition), Dec. 19, 1956, p. 8. Letter in answer to an attack by Lonnquist published in a previous issue of the newspaper.

"Letters to Joe C. Brown," edited with an introduction by Thomas Knipp, Kent State University Libraries, Kent, Ohio, 1968, 12 p. This is an unauthorized edition whose circulation has been prohibited by Mrs. Ellen Wright. [8 letters from 1938 to 1945]

NOTES ON CONTRIBUTORS

DANIEL AARON, Director of American Studies at Smith College, has published several books, including *Men of Good Hope.*

MARGARET WALKER ALEXANDER'S *Jubilee* was a Houghton Mifflin Literary Fellowship Award Novel, and was proclaimed widely as "the reverse side of *Gone With the Wind.*"

BENJAMIN APPEL published his first novel, *Brain Guy,* in 1934, and his fifteenth, *A Signature of Love,* will appear in 1972; he now lives in Roosevelt, N. J., and has worked as an aviation mechanic, ghost speech writer, and historian on the U. S. Mission to the Philippines.

HARRY BIRDOFF sent his letter from New York.

HORACE CAYTON was a noted Black writer, whose autobiography *Long Old Road,* appeared in 1963.

JACK CONROY, who resides in Moberly, Missouri, edited the magazines he mentions in his article, and was a central figure in proletarian literature of the thirties and forties; his *The Disinherited* is considered a classic.

THOMAS CRIPPS, a Morgan State College historian who has taught at Stanford and elsewhere, has spent years studying the portrait of Blacks in the movies.

MORRIS DICKSTEIN teaches at Queens College, and contributes to such magazines as *Partisan Review*; his essay here is part of a longer study.

OWEN DODSON has written many plays and a novel, *When Trees Were Green,* as well as a book of poems, *Powerful Long Ladder.*

MICHEL FABRE, professor at the Sorbonne, is perhaps the world's leading scholar in matters concerning Richard Wright.

ROBERT M. FARNSWORTH edited *The Conjure Woman* and *The Wife of His Youth and Other Stories,* volumes by Charles Chesnutt, for the University of Michigan Press.

MICHAEL HARPER is author of two volumes of poetry, the most recent being *History Is Your Own Heartbeat.*

JOHN HOUSEMAN's essay is from his forthcoming autobiography, *Run-Through* (Simon & Schuster); he is one of America's most distinguished producers and directors.

EDWARD MARGOLIES is the author of *The Art of Richard Wright.*

LLOYD J. REYNOLDS is the noted calligrapher who lives in Portland, Oregon.

FRANK SAFFORD, M.D., dictated his thoughts about Richard Wright to Elizabeth Hill Downey, who describes Dr. Safford as "a leader of a most interesting commune in the '40s."

KATHERINE SPRANDEL is completing a thesis on Richard Wright at Michigan State University.

WINBURN T. THOMAS is a noted clergyman who has been active as a missionary; his *Protestant Beginnings in Japan* is available from Charles E. Tuttle Company.

EDWARD A. WATSON, of the University of Windsor, has published many critical articles, and has a book forthcoming from Princeton University Press.

HENRIETTA WEIGEL's novel, *Age of Doom,* was published by E. P. Dutton in 1947, and many of her short stories have appeared in such anthologies as *The Best American Short Stories.*

GRACE McSPADDEN WHITE was a participant at last summer's University of Iowa conference on Richard Wright; she teaches at St. Andrews Presbyterian College.

SIDNEY WILLIAMS, who conducts an African import business in Chicago, was a good friend of Richard Wright and Horace Cayton.